I0877791

THE *Dark Side of* JANE AUSTEN'S WORLD

THE *Dark Side of* JANE AUSTEN'S WORLD

ANGELA YOUNGMAN

PEN & SWORD
HISTORY
AN IMPRINT OF PEN & SWORD BOOKS LTD.
YORKSHIRE – PHILADELPHIA

First published in Great Britain in 2024 by
Pen & Sword History
An imprint of
Pen & Sword Books Ltd
Yorkshire - Philadelphia

ISBN 978 1 39908 084 2

A CIP catalogue record for this book is available from the British Library.

Typeset in INDIA by IMPEC eSolutions
Printed and bound in England by CPI (UK) Ltd.

Pen & Sword Books Limited incorporates the imprints of Archaeology, Atlas, Aviation, Battleground, Digital, Discovery, Family History, Fiction, History, Local, Local History, Maritime, Military, Military Classics, Politics, Select, Transport, True Crime, After the Battle, Air World, Claymore Press, Frontline Publishing, Leo Cooper, Remember When, Seaforth Publishing, The Praetorian Press, Wharncliffe Books, Wharncliffe Local History, Wharncliffe Transport, Wharncliffe True Crime and White Owl.

For a complete list of Pen & Sword titles please contact

PEN & SWORD BOOKS LIMITED
47 Church Street, Barnsley, South Yorkshire, S70 2AS, England
E-mail: enquiries@pen-and-sword.co.uk
Website: www.pen-and-sword.co.uk

or

PEN AND SWORD BOOKS
1950 Lawrence Rd, Havertown, PA 19083, USA
E-mail: uspen-and-sword@casematepublishers.com
Website: www.penandswordbooks.com

FSC www.fsc.org MIX Paper | Supporting responsible forestry FSC® C013604

Contents

Introduction: The Hidden Darkness

Jane Austen, the unassuming, unmarried daughter of a rural clergyman living in Regency England, wrote only a handful of books, but her influence has far exceeded anything she might have anticipated. Her books are read worldwide and have spawned an industry of their own, covering everything from merchandise to millions of internet sites. Over the years, both Jane Austen and her books have become a multi-million-pound industry and have taken some extremely unexpected directions, including excursions into pornography and horror.

Of all her books, one in particular stands out; *Pride and Prejudice*, which has been described as 'the most romantic novel ever written', with Darcy being 'the most romantic hero'. As Susannah Fullerton points out in her book *Happily Ever After*:

> After 200 years, it has become a truth universally acknowledged that no book is more loved. Again and again in so many countries, it tops the polls as the favourite novel of all time. It is read and studied in China; there are Jane Austen societies appreciating it around the world, even in non-English speaking countries … University theses are written about it in Sweden … Facebook has an International Pride and Prejudice Day … Newspapers around the world regularly use the phrases 'pride and prejudice' and 'truth universally acknowledged' to grab attention. The [book's] first sentence has become 'universal'

> property. No other sentence from literature has been paid the compliment of such excessive imitation.

Reasons for this popularity are not hard to find. These are stories that capture the imagination, encourage readers to explore her world and feel at home in it. The gentle humour and character insights are appealing, with storylines that never fail to engage. Her books were surprisingly innovative as she utilised a unique writing style blending first-person narrative speech with third-person storytelling. Her characters rarely use direct conversation, but readers still instantly understand what they say and think. During the First World War, *Pride and Prejudice* often appeared on the 'fever chart' for sick and wounded in hospitals because it was seen as a comfort book. For the same reason it was often read by soldiers in the trenches; we know, for example, that Siegfried Sassoon read *Pride and Prejudice* to help him relax between battles.

All her books are lively and entertaining. The storylines are complex, yet can be easily followed, portraying a relaxed community with its own distinct social organisation. But below the froth and romance, other stories are wating to be discovered.

By looking below the surface, it is possible to identify the darker side of Regency and Georgian society, including the issues presented by the opium trade and slavery. Marriage bore serious risks; losing your status was a frightening prospect, and lack of property to provide security a permanent nightmare. The threat of poverty was always present. This was a world in which people faced deadly diseases, adulterated food, and the ever-present risk of becoming a victim of crime. Punishments were severe and could involve death or transportation for even the smallest of crimes. Jane's aunt faced the real risk being forcibly transported to Australia after being accused of stealing ribbon. Even though she was acquitted, Mrs Leigh-Perrot still spent many months in prison.

Younger sons might never be able to marry in a world where ownership of land and property was dominant, leaving them rootless and struggling to find a career. Every woman faced the overwhelming problem of trying to find a husband, survive marriage or find some way of surviving as a single woman with very few potential opportunities outside marriage. This was a world in which social disorder was rife, and the chances of a long life were extremely low.

Chapter 1

Land, Power and Family

Land equalled power and status in Jane Austen's world, underpinning all aspects of society. People possessing land and an income that came from it were automatically deemed to have a higher status in society. Successful professional and tradespeople only achieved a significant social standing when they acquired an estate. When Mrs Bennett in *Pride and Prejudice* refers to Mr Darcy as having an income of £10,000 per year, it related to his income from rents and farming.

In most cases, land and property were inherited – a situation that instantly posed problems for women within the eighteenth and nineteenth centuries. The death of a husband or father could leave them homeless, and virtually destitute. Even if their father was a landowner, and they were the only direct heirs, there was no guarantee they could inherit.

Since the thirteenth century, land ownership within England, Scotland and Wales had passed through the male line. Primogeniture was the norm. Every landowner wanted a son, preferably several sons, to secure the line of inheritance. The oldest son would automatically inherit unless he died before his father, in which case the next son would then become heir. This ensured that all the land in an estate stayed within one family. Unless required to inherit the property, other sons would generally enter the Church, seek a military career, or enter the law, then potentially receive a cash sum on the death of their father. It was expected that the sons would assume responsibility for the wellbeing of their mother and any sisters.

If there were no sons, then the eldest daughter might be able to inherit – but she would experience very limited rights. Control over their income was in the hands of trustees. Heiresses became the target of fortune hunters, seeking access to their money and land. As soon as they married, the husband gained control. Under the law, married women were regarded as being bound by coverture, which regarded a married couple as one economic unit.

Explaining the nature of coverture, Jurist William Blackstone wrote in his 1765 *Commentaries on the Laws of England*:

> By marriage, the husband and wife are one person in law; the very being or legal existence of the woman is suspended during the marriage, or at least is incorporated and consolidated into that of the husband … and her condition during her marriage is called her coverture.
>
> … For this reason, a man cannot grant anything to his wife, or enter into covenant with her: for the grant would be to suppose her separate existence; and to covenant with her, would be only to covenant with himself … a husband may also bequeath any thing to his wife by will; for that cannot take effect till the coverture is determined by his death.

Interestingly, while married, a wife could not be sued. If she ran up debts and the husband could not pay, then her husband went to the debtors' prison, but she would remain at liberty.

Above all, the husband controlled all property and personal assets, as well as any rental income from property belonging to his wife, who could not sell or rent it without his permission. Under such circumstances, the land would have passed out of one family into another.

To avoid this problem, land ownership inheritance laws often included entails, limiting inheritance to specific people and enabling the land to stay within the family. Under the terms of an entail, if there were no direct male descendants, the property would pass to the nearest male relative, which meant that wives and daughters could find themselves with no income and no inheritance if no marriage settlement had been made.

This is exactly the situation faced by the Dashwoods in *Sense and Sensibility*. Mrs Dashwood was her husband's second wife, and he had not lived long enough to save money to bestow on the daughters of his second marriage. When he died, they only had their mother's dowry and the personal possessions she had brought to the marriage.

A similar situation faced the Bennetts in *Pride and Prejudice*, where an entail existed on the family property. Mr Bennett had always thought he would have a son, and so had made no allowances for having only girls. He tells Mrs Bennett:

> 'I received this letter ... it is from my cousin, Mr Collins, who, when I am dead, may turn you all out of this house as soon as he pleases.'
>
> 'Oh! my dear,' cried his wife, 'I cannot bear to hear that mentioned. Pray do not talk of that odious man. I do think it is the hardest thing in the world that your estate should be entailed away from your own children; and I am sure if I had been you, I should have tried long ago to do something or other about it.'

The existence of entails did come in for criticism. In *Pride and Prejudice*, we see Lady Catherine de Bourgh deriding the practice of excluding the female line from inheritance saying, 'I see no occasion for entailing estates from the female line – it was not thought necessary in Sir Lewis de Bourgh's family.'

For some childless landowners, adoption was regarded as a solution to the issue, and generally involved a male child from a subsidiary branch of the family, and this is exactly what happened within Jane Austen's own family.

Thomas Knight, a wealthy landowner in Kent, was Mr Austen's cousin. He and his wife, Catherine, came to visit the Austen's at Steventon Parsonage while on their wedding journey, and during the visit they met Mr Austen's oldest son, Edward, who was at that time 12 years old. It was later reported that they 'were first attracted by his personal beauty' and that he possessed a 'spirit of fun and liveliness'. They decided to take him with them on the rest of their journey – a common practice of the period – returning him to the Rectory afterwards.

Contact between the two families continued, and the Knights invited Edward to stay with them now and again. Since the Knight's marriage proved childless, Mrs Austen regarded their interest as something to be encouraged. Eventually, the Knights asked him to stay permanently as their adopted son and heir, with Mrs Austen telling her husband 'I think, my Dear, you had better oblige your cousin, and let the Child go.'

Thus, in 1783, aged 16, Edward was officially handed over to his new family. It was a shrewd move since it provided Edward with the prospect of inheriting land and property, and ultimately achieving a position where he could help his mother and sisters. There can be little doubt that Edward gained significantly from the adoption, especially given he was sent to complete his education via a Grand Tour of Europe. In 1786 he spent a month in Switzerland, followed by a visit to Italy, before returning to Switzerland, Germany and the Netherlands four years later. He then focused on learning to manage the Knight estates in preparation for eventually taking them over.

The concept of adoption as a form of inheritance appeared in Jane Austen's novels. In *Emma*, Frank Churchill was informally adopted by the childless brother of his deceased mother, while in *Mansfield Park*, Fanny Price is informally adopted by her aunt and uncle in order to help her impoverished parents.

Such adoptions were sometimes challenged when the adoptee inherited estates. Edward Austen inherited the estates of Chawton, Godmersham and Winchester from Thomas Knight on the condition that he changed his surname to Knight. Thomas Knight's will confirmed Edward's official adoption, but this did not prevent challenges to his inheritance, which caused some financial problems. In 1814, Edward's adoption and ownership of the Knight properties was challenged by a consortium centred around James Baverstock. Their challenge was based on a legal document dating back to the granting of the Hampshire estates to Thomas Brodnax-May-Knight of Godmersham. The Hinton family had been named as heirs if the Knight line ended. Baverstock's argument was that Edward was not a blood relative, just an adopted one, and therefore the Knight line had ended and the estates should go elsewhere. The situation was only settled after several years of legal arguments and the payment of £15,000 to the claimants.

There was some recognition of the potentially dire situation that could face females when the husband or father died. Attempts were made to provide some long-term support. Much depended on the strength of the settlement arranged before a marriage could take place. These settlements were organised as a result of discussions between the two families and their respective lawyers and related to a woman's dowry, as well as money and or land settled on her by her prospective husband. Negotiations for a marriage settlement could take months to arrange, and it was not unknown for engagements to be ended if a settlement could not be reached. Even ordinary families often tried to safeguard a daughter's rights by insisting on written settlements, likewise widows accepting a second marriage.

If an elopement took place, then the woman lost all security. This was one of the reasons why 16-year-old Lydia Bennet's decision to elope with George Wickham in *Pride and Prejudice* was regarded as disastrous. Without a settlement, George Wickham could have simply used up what little fortune Lydia had, leaving her totally penniless.

A similar situation existed if a widow remarried and did not arrange a settlement in advance, as can be seen at the beginning of *Sense and Sensibility*, where Mrs Dashwood is reduced to instant penury.

Property laws also affected the status of a woman within a marriage. A married woman was regarded as the property of their husband. Dr Johnson pointed out that 'All the property of the world depends on female chastity' and that 'confusion of progeny constitutes the essence of the crime of adultery'.

As a result, if a woman committed adultery it was regarded as a question of property, ownership and contract breaking affecting the husband's honour. This was referred to as a 'criminal conversation' and could be used as evidence in divorce proceedings. Husbands such as Mr Rushworth in *Mansfield Park* were able to take their wife's lover to court and successfully sue for damages to their property, on the basis that the wife's body was being used by another man. If she eloped with her lover, then the husband could claim for loss of a housekeeper. When awarding damages, the jury had to consider rank and fortune, how long the couple had been married, if the husband and the wife's lover had been friends, how long the wife had been committing adultery and the exact location where the adultery (described as the 'outrage') took place. If the wife and her lover had committed the 'outrage' within the marital bed, then damages would be even higher.

In 1776, John Craven, the uncle of Jane Austen's friends Martha and Mary Lloyd, was cited in a 'criminal conversation' by Mr John Potter Harris, of Baughurst in Hampshire. John Craven was said to have committed adultery with Mrs Harris, and as a result had to pay Mr Harris £3,000 in damages.

In 1788, the Lord Chief Justice Lord Kenyon consistently awarded husbands high damages in such cases. This had the result of encouraging husbands in need of money to deliberately incriminate their wives on the basis that 'criminal conversations' would be a good way to gain cash. One such husband is reported to have commented 'as most of us bargain to be husbands, so some of us bargain to be cuckolds' and that aged husbands married young women in order to make money from adultery.

When getting married, women – particularly from the gentry and aristocracy – received a marriage portion from their families. This was effectively a dowry and comprised a lump sum of money that she brought to the marriage. It was expected that this would be returned to her when her husband died and ultimately divided among any daughters on her death. The size of the marriage portion could vary tremendously. In 1733, Parliament granted Princess Anne, the oldest daughter of George II, a marriage portion of £80,000. Warren Hastings settled £10,000 on his 'goddaughter' Eliza, who may well have been his illegitimate child, which would act as a dowry and also provide long term support so that she 'would not be under the necessity of marrying a Tradesman, or any Man for her support.' In *Pride and Prejudice*, Mrs Bennett brought £5,000 to the marriage as her dowry. On her death, her daughters would receive £1,000 each. In addition, the settlement could stipulate specific sums for 'pin money' to provide payment for clothing and pocket money.

Although the majority of marriage settlements were made among the gentry and aristocracy, there are examples of marriage settlements being made at other levels of society. On 30 January 1755, William Lucas, a carpenter living in Hitchen, signed an agreement relating to his marriage to Mary Blow, daughter of Thomas Blow of Stevenage. Like Lucas, Thomas Blow was a carpenter. The agreement was designed to make a 'competent jointure' for Mary Blow (who was unable to sign her name) and provision for any children of the marriage if she survived him. The agreement was 'in recompense barr and satisfaction of all dower and thirds which she hath … or may claim'. It related to property that Lucas had inherited from his grandfather, Simon Lucas, as well as the Maltings in Bancroft Street, Hitchen in which Lucas and Mary Blow were then living. The property was placed in the hands of his father-in-law for the nominal sum of 5 shillings. This gave Mary Blow some long-term protection in the event of her husband's death or being forced into bankruptcy.

Settlements involving large landowners could be very complex, as can be seen from the negotiations relating to the marriage of Augusta Ada Byron (1815-52) and William Lord King (1805-93), who ultimately became the 1st Earl of Lovelace. The settlement was complicated, covering land in five counties, and required the approval of the Courts of Chancery since Ada had been made a Ward of Chancery in order to protect her from any claim that her 'mad, bad and dangerous to know' father – Lord Byron – might make. The legal documents involved were huge not just in terms of the detail but also in sheer weight; main conveyances weighed 7lb 7oz (3.5 kg). A further ten documents were needed before and after the marriage in order to deal with final arrangements. Ada brought a dowry of £30,000 to the marriage, plus the possibility of future inheritance if the reversion of her mother's rights to the Barony of Wentworth and its Leicestershire lands could be arranged. William King provided over 9,000 acres of land in Surrey, Somerset, Devon and Dorset, with 200 tenant farmers and rental properties to support their married life. In addition, the settlement set out that Ada Byron would receive pin money amounting to £600 per annum from both the King and Wentworth estates.

On marrying, all monies and land, apart from the dowry, became the property of a woman's husband under the rules of coverture. The wife could take personal property such as furniture to her new home, which then became the property of her husband – but all of it had to be returned to her at his death.

The settlement could also include a jointure as an alternative to a widow's share. Widows had the right to a dower share, or one third of her husband's estate, which could involve income from a farm or rental property. A jointure was a sum of money based on assets and the money the wife had brought to the marriage. The wife would receive this money on an annual basis after her husband died. It could not be passed to her daughters and the annual payments would cease on her death. Likewise, a widow's share could not be sold or bequeathed.

Arrangements could be negotiated between the male heir and the widow. Frequently, the widow went to live in a Dower House on an estate. When Jane Austen's relative Mr Knight died, her brother Edward took over the management of the estates. Mrs Knight decided to live in Canterbury, leaving Godmersham Park as Edward's home in return for an annual income of £1,000. This money would be paid out of the profits of the estates, but if the estate encountered problems at any point Edward would be faced with having to pay Mrs Knight £1,000 each year from his own income.

The importance of a marriage settlement such as this can be seen in *Persuasion*. Lady Russell chooses not to remarry after her husband's death in order to protect her financial status. Her widow's dower rights combined with her dowry provides her with sufficient income on which to live and allow her to control her own money and possessions. If she had remarried, she would have immediately lost her widow's dower rights.

Lady Russell's financial position was unusual – most women on entering widowhood encountered immediate problems. Together with their daughters, they could be quickly made homeless when the new owners of an estate or property arrived. Yearly income from dowries could be quite small. In *Pride and Prejudice*, Mrs Bennett had a £5,000 marriage settlement, which would have given her just £200 per year based on an interest of 4 percent. All too frequently, widows and daughters had to rely on charity from other members of the family.

Annuities were often arranged in the form of a guaranteed sum of money to be paid annually by family members. After the Reverend

George Austen's death in 1805, Jane Austen's brothers arranged an annuity payable to their mother and sisters in order to provide an adequate income. Edward and Frank jointly provided £150 per annum, while James and Henry added a further £50 each per annum, giving a total sum of £250. Henry and James admitted that providing this sum was difficult for them, but Henry promised to 'do as much as long as [his] precarious income remains'. In 1816, Henry had to stop paying his share due to the fact he had been declared bankrupt. Luckily, their eldest brother, Edward Knight, now the owner of several estates, was able to provide them with a house in which to live.

A far less happy fate awaited Mrs Dashwood and her daughters in *Sense and Sensibility*. When her husband dies, his son from an earlier marriage automatically inherits the family house and land at Norland Park, and Mrs Dashwood and her daughters have little choice but to move out. Apart from her dowry and possessions, they have no income. The new owners, John and Fanny Dashwood, discuss ways in which they could meet his father's request to care for them. Setting up an annuity is one option, which soon gets dismissed when they consider the implications.

> [John Dashwood]: '… I do not know whether … it would not be more advisable to do something for their mother while she lives, rather than for them – something of the annuity kind I mean. My sisters would feel the good effects of it as well as herself. A hundred a year would make them all perfectly comfortable.'
>
> His wife hesitated a little, however, in giving her consent to this plan.
>
> 'To be sure,' said she, 'it is better than parting with fifteen hundred pounds at once. But then if Mrs Dashwood should live fifteen years, we shall be completely taken in.'

> 'Fifteen years! My dear Fanny, her life cannot be worth half that purchase.'
>
> 'Certainly not; but if you observe, people always live for ever when there is any annuity be paid them.'

Fanny then explains the reasons behind her argument.

> An annuity is a very serious business; it comes over and over every year, and there is no getting rid of it … I have known a great deal of the trouble of annuities; for my mother was clogged with the payment of three to old, superannuated servants by my father's will, and it is amazing how disagreeable she found it. Twice every year these annuities were to be paid; and then there was the trouble of getting it to them; and then one of them was said to have died, and afterwards it turned out to be no such thing. My mother was quite sick of it. Her income was not her own, she said, with such perpetual claims on it; and it was the more unkind in my father, because, otherwise, the money would have been entirely at my mother's disposal, without any restriction whatsoever. It has given me such an abhorrence of annuities, that I am sure I would not pin myself down to the payment of one for all the world.

Thanks to his wife's persuasion, John Dashwood decides in favour of granting £50 to his step-mother and step-sisters now and again since this would provide them with enough to live on, thus fulfilling his promise to his father.

As a result of these inheritance issues, and the problems of finding an income, many Georgian families were assiduous legacy hunters, making the most of every family connection in the hope of acquiring a legacy. If possessing suitable connections, impecunious families, especially widows and their daughters, would frequently spend several months each year travelling around the country to stay with relatives. This enabled them to cement family connections, meet other family members, and above all, make themselves well-known to people who had the means to leave legacies. Such stays also helped budgeting as it meant free lodging and entertainment for several weeks. All too frequently, legacy hunting was met with disappointment.

The Austen family were no exception to this. As a young orphan, the Reverend George Austen had been able to develop a career in the church and gain the necessary education to do this via the help provided by his rich uncle, Francis Austen, who lived in Sevenoaks. Over the years, contact between the two families was maintained, but when George Austen's uncle, known as 'Old Francis', died in 1791, Mr Austen was disappointed to only receive £500 in the will. Francis Austen had left most of his wealth to his already wealthy eldest son and had even excluded the niece who had kept house for him for many years. As Lucy Worsley points out *Jane Austen at Home*, 'When the crunch came, primogeniture overwhelmed any feelings of fairness or charity.'

When Jane Austen's father decided to retire from his living at Steventon, he took his family to Bath, regarding this as the ideal retirement location. It was a decision that resulted in a major drop in income, as by giving up the living and the farm, the Reverend Austen's income was now just £600 per annum. Another good reason for choosing Bath was the fact that the family had connections there. Mrs Austen's wealthy brother, James Leigh-Perrot, and his wife spent their winters in Bath. Indeed, Jane had been sent to stay with them for a season in 1797 as a way of meeting potential suitors. By moving to Bath, the Austen family could take advantage of the presence of their relatives and stay with them at their home at No 1 The Paragon, while house hunting. They knew James' wife could be difficult to live with (the two families had stayed in each other's homes before, and

Jane had stayed with the Leigh-Perrots on a previous visit to Bath), but were prepared to cope with it for the time being. In one of Jane's letters to Cassandra, she refers to a nasty letter from her aunt Leigh-Perrot, 'the discontentedness of it shocked and surprised … I see nothing in it out of nature – tho' a sad nature'.

James Leigh-Perrot was Mrs Austen's only surviving brother and had the power to eventually provide them with a good legacy. Many years earlier, James Leigh-Perrot had inherited an estate from a childless relative, while his wife was a wealthy West Indian heiress. As the Leigh-Perrots were childless and so closely linked by birth to Mrs Austen, the prospect of legacies loomed on the horizon. Not surprisingly, Jane wrote that the Austens would 'avoid anything that might seem a slight to them'.

Even the daily socialising in Bath was affected by this continual interest in potential legacies and connections. Families like the Austens would meet a constantly changing group of people, many of whom had come just to take the waters for a while. Everyone was instinctively aware that every conversation in the Pump Room, at balls and other events might lead to a useful connection and possibly even a legacy in time. Such social links led to Jane and Cassandra Austen receiving a small legacy from Mrs Leigh-Perrot's widowed friend, Mrs Lillington, who gave them each £50 in her will, reflecting the time they had spent socialising with her. Legacy hunting was serious business.

The death of Mr George Austen in 1805 signalled not only more financial problems for the Austen family, but an even greater interest in the possibilities of legacies. When Mr Austen died, the family's income immediately dropped dramatically, and they could no longer count on any income from Steventon. Mrs Austen had an annual income of £122 from a family inheritance of £3,350 invested in the South Sea Company. Cassandra received a yearly interest on the £1,000 she had inherited from her fiancé, Tom Fowle, who had accompanied his friend Lord Craven to the West Indies as chaplain but had sadly died en route. This additional money resulted in a combined family income of £210 per annum. The girls had been left nothing in their father's will – everything he had went to his wife. They were now dependent on charity from their brothers. This meant that given the size of the annuities their brothers were able to provide, Mrs Austen and her daughters had a combined household income of £460.

As a result, the women were forced to economise. Henry wrote to his brother Frank that his mother would 'reduce her establishment to one female domestic and take furnished lodgings' and that 'she will be very comfortable. A small establishment will be as agreeable to them … I really think that My Mother and Sisters will be to the full as ever. They will not only suffer no personal deprivation but will be able to pay occasional visits of health and pleasure to their friends.'

The prospect of obtaining a legacy was very much to the forefront of the girls' visit to relatives in July/August 1806. They went to stay with Mrs Austen's cousin, the Reverend Thomas Leigh, at Adlestrop, Stow-on-the-Wold in Gloucestershire. Thomas Leigh lived in the Rectory, while his nephew James Leigh occupied Adlestrop House.

Their stay at Adlestrop was very short as Thomas Leigh was involved with settling the estate of a wealthy relative, the Honourable Mrs Mary Leigh. Mary Leigh had been helpful to the Austen family over the years, having given Jane's brother James his two livings, sinecures as absentee curates, as well as £200 for the care of Mrs Austen's disabled brother. Her death was seen as a good opportunity to remind Thomas Leigh of the Austen's precarious position – a widow with two unmarried daughters, neither possessing dowries. Jane wrote a letter to Cassandra stating, 'I do not know where we are to get our Legacy, but we will keep a sharp look-out'.

The Austens accompanied Thomas Leigh, his unmarried sister, and the family lawyer Joseph Hill to Stoneleigh Abbey on 5 August. Other impoverished relatives were also quick to appear; Stoneleigh was a very desirable property and it was uncertain as to who would be the eventual inheritor.

The estate had come into the control of Thomas Leigh, Lord Mayor of London during the Tudor period. Thomas Leigh had nine children by his wife, and many of his descendants had prospered. The estate had passed directly from father to son seven times. In 1767, the fifth Lord Leigh wrote his will as he was about to go on a Grand Tour of Europe. He had no wife or children and so he left everything to his sister Mary. Lord Leigh returned from his Grand Tour as 'a Lunatick of unsound mind' and never recovered. On his death in 1786, the estate went to his sister for her lifetime and then, according to his will, was to go to 'the first and nearest of his kindred, being male and of his blood and name.'

Unfortunately, he did not name specific heirs. Several junior members added Leigh to their surnames in the hope of benefiting in some way. The two strongest contenders were the Reverend Thomas Leigh and James Leigh-Perrot. There were suggestions at the time that Mrs Leigh-Perrot was the main reason why James Leigh-Perrot was pursuing his claim since he was prepared to give up any claim in return for a down payment. In the ensuing negotiations, James Leigh-Perrot indicated he would give up his claim in return for £20,000 plus an annual annuity of £2,000. The Reverend Thomas Leigh proposed that James Leigh-Perrot's share should include provision for Mrs Austen and her daughters, Jane and Cassandra. The family lawyer recommended that £8,000 of that share be settled on the Austen family. James Leigh-Perrot opposed this.

On 14 August, the Austen's left Stoneleigh to visit their Cooper relatives at Hemstell Ridware, Staffordshire before heading to join Frank Austen and his new wife, Mary, in Southampton. On 3 September, the lawyers contacted the Austens to say that Mary Leigh had left Cassandra and Jane each 'a single brilliant centre ring worth 5 guineas'. The Austen family continued to have hopes of something from the final settlement commenting that 'A legacy is our sovereign good.' Both the Reverend Thomas Leigh and James Leigh-Perrot were wealthy and in their seventies. They were to be disappointed.

The saga of Stoneleigh continued to resound among the Austen family and friends, coming in for considerable criticism. When the Reverend Thomas Austen died, Jane wrote that 'Poor Mrs Leigh-Perrot, who would now have been Mistress of Stoneleigh had there been none of that vile compromise which in good truth has never been allowed to be of much good to them – it will be a hard trial.'

Jane and her siblings (apart from James) received nothing. No legacy appeared, even though, under the Reverend Austen's nephew's care, the Stoneleigh estate became even more prosperous. By the mid nineteenth century, the Stoneleigh estate was bringing in over £30,000 a year and was the largest landowner in Victorian Warwickshire.

Chapter 2

Education and Fashion for Young Girls

Growing up in the late eighteenth and early nineteenth centuries was not easy, especially if you were a girl from a gentrified or aristocratic family. A girl's future was mapped out almost from birth, where she was expected to learn social and household skills designed to make her a suitable wife and mother in due course. Above all, girls had to learn how to run a household and organise the servants. This role is clearly portrayed in *Pride and Prejudice*, where Mrs Bennet is clearly shown to be the mistress in her own home, capable of undertaking all the basic requirements of a good hostess. Her home is comfortable and welcoming to guests, with good food always available. Discussing a meal, Mrs Bennet notes that 'the venison was roasted to a turn … the soup was fifty times better than what we had at the Lucas's.' On another occasion when she discovers that fish was not available, she quickly goes to speak to Mrs Hill (the housekeeper) to discuss menus. The Bennet daughters have been brought up knowing how to behave in society, and how to organise a household and manage servants. This is seen after Lydia's elopement with George Wickham, when Mrs Bennet is overcome with distress and Jane Bennet is immediately able to take charge of the household in her place.

There were many books available providing advice, especially on etiquette and behaviour. It has been estimated that between 59,000 and 119,000 books of this kind were sold between 1785-1820. One such book, frequently mentioned in *Pride and Prejudice*, was *Sermons to Young Women* by James Fordyce, a copy of which was kept in the library at Godmersham Park. Fordyce recommended girls to dress modestly, to be meek and virtuous, as well as acquiring domestic, intellectual and social accomplishments. Above all, they should learn all that would make themselves useful and agreeable to men. 'If aught on earth can present the image of celestial excellence in its softest array, it is surely an accomplished Woman, in whom purity and meekness, intelligence and modesty, mingle their charms,' Fordyce wrote. The book was frequently quoted by Mr Collins to illustrate his beliefs of how females should behave, but the Bennet girls were far less keen and possessed little desire to read it!

Another popular book was *Mentoria: or, the Young Ladies Instructor* by Ann Murry, which was dedicated to the Princess Royal. Initially published in 1778, it covers a range of topics including politeness, civility, truth, Sabbath observance, the duties of life, grammar, arithmetic, geography and history. It was certainly known to Jane Austen; there is a copy in existence at her home at Chawton that is clearly inscribed 'Jane Anna Elizabeth Austen 1801. From her Aunt Jane.' Jane Anna would have been around 7 years old when she received the book. She was the daughter of Jane's eldest brother James and his first wife, Anne Mathew. Given that there is another, earlier inscription on the inside cover that reads, 'Jane Austen June 29th 1785', it is very likely that this is Jane's own childhood copy of the book and she had passed it on to her niece while sorting out her books ready for her move to Bath.

In 1805, Jane wrote to Cassandra that 'I am glad you recommended Gisborne, for having begun, I am pleased with it, and I had quite determined not to read it.' She was referring to Thomas Gisborne's *An Enquiry into the Duties of the Female Sex*. Written by a clergyman, it covered a range of topics including female education, choosing a husband, raising children, the differences between men and women and how women should spend their free time. Unlike Fordyce's *Sermons*, which stressed the need for modesty and submissiveness,

Gisborne highlights the importance of women's 'sprightliness and vivacity', 'quickness of perception' and 'fertility of invention'.

Unlike girls, boys would receive an education from a tutor before being sent to schools like Eton, Winchester and other smaller institutions. There they would study a classical education focusing primarily on Latin, Greek and scripture, along with opportunities to obtain social skills like dancing and fencing. Clergymen's sons were often sent off to be educated in small schools set up by other clergy within their homes. Jane's father, the Reverend George Austen, was one such cleric who supplemented his income by tutoring a group of boys to prepare them for university, making room in his home for them by sending his daughters off to boarding school.

A girl's education was much more limited, with the aim of developing girls capable of succeeding in the marriage mart and becoming wives and mothers. It was an education that came under some criticism from writers such as Mary Wollstonecraft, Catharine Macaulay and Hannah More. In her *Letters on Education*, dated 1790, Catharine Macaulay advised that parents 'confine not the education of your daughters to what is regarded as the ornamental parts of it'. Another writer, Hester Chapone, advocated extensive reading programmes of which 'the principal study ... is history. I know of nothing equally proper to entertain and improve at the same time, or that is so likely to form and strengthen your judgement.'

Many girls were educated at home by a governess or were sent at an early age to one of the many small boarding schools for young ladies appearing across the country. These schools often catered for approximately twenty or more girls, usually from about 7 to 15 years old. Life could be strict and monotonous, with lessons focusing on subjects such as English, needlework, dancing, music, drawing and, if they were lucky, a little history and geography. Conditions ranged from spartan to luxurious and it was hit or miss as to which type of school or level of education would be encountered.

The Bennett sisters in *Pride and Prejudice* were educated at home and were left very much to their own devices, as Elizabeth indicates when talking to Lady Catherine de Burgh. 'Compared with some families, I believe we were [neglected]; but such of us as wished to learn never wanted the means. We were always encouraged to read, and had all the masters that were necessary. Those who chose to be idle, certainly might.' Elizabeth does, however, admit to having only a few accomplishments, such as being able to play the piano a little, but not being able to draw. It was an upbringing that shocked Lady Catherine.

A similar situation is encountered in *Northanger Abbey*. Catherine Morland's education was supervised by her mother, who was said to be, 'so much occupied in lying-in and teaching the little ones, that her elder daughters were inevitably left to shift for themselves.' Catherine was not really interested in learning, being 'often inattentive and occasionally stupid', but learned the fable of *The Hare and Many Friends* 'as quickly as any girl in England'.

Taught by a governess who is more a friend than a teacher, Emma Woodhouse's education was by no means thorough. The family friend Mr Knightley attempts to amend this by encouraging her to read widely, but discovers she spends more time making lists of books than actually reading them. He comments that this is a serious flaw in her development since 'she will never submit to anything requiring industry and patience, and a subjection of the fancy to the understanding.' And although the Bertram sisters in *Mansfield Park* have a governess, there is little interest in developing their education since 'to the education of her daughters, Lady Bertram paid not the smallest attention. She had not time for such cares.' Sir Thomas Bertram is equally limited in his interest since all he is concerned about is that they 'exercise their memories, practise their duets, and grow tall and womanly.'

In *Persuasion*, Anne Elliot attends a school with a strict timetable: up at 6am, prayers at 7.30, breakfast at 8, then writing and other subjects until 4pm followed by sewing. At 6pm they drank tea, prepared lessons and played. At 7.30 the girls had a meal of bread, cheese and beer, before prayers at 8pm followed by bed. Drawing lessons were given on Tuesdays and Fridays, and dancing on Wednesdays.

A more general overview of life for girls at school and what was expected of them there is provided in *Emma*:

> Mrs Goddard was the mistress of a school – not of a seminary, or an establishment, or any thing which professed, in long sentences of refined nonsense, to combine liberal acquirements with elegant morality, upon new principles and new systems – and where young ladies for enormous pay might be screwed out of health and into vanity – but a real, honest, old-fashioned boarding school, where a reasonable quantity of accomplishments were sold at a reasonable price, and where girls might be sent to be out of the way, and scramble themselves into a little education, without any danger of coming back prodigies.

Such attitudes were common. Writing to her sister Sarah in 1773, Mrs Elizabeth Montague, a prominent intellectual and member of the Bluestocking movement, commented:

> I am glad you intend to send my eldest niece to a boarding school. What girls learn at these schools is trifling, but they unlearn what would be a great disservice – a provincial dialect, which is extremely ungenteel, and other tricks that they learn in the nursery. The carriage of the person, which is of great importance, is well attended to, and dancing is well taught. As for the French language, I do not think it is necessary, unless for persons in very high life. It is rarely much cultivated at school. I believe all the boarding-schools are much on the same plan, so that you may place the young lady wherever there is good air and a good dancing master.

In 1786, Sophie La Roche described her visit to a girls' school in Queen's Square, London. This was one of the larger schools since it had 220 pupils, each girl paying fees of around 100 guineas annually: 'A liveried attendant led us from the pretty hall into the visitors room where the damask draperies, fine lustres fitted to the wall, mirrors and two sofas in every way resembled the interior of a wealthy home.'

She watched a group of girls clad in white, with red, blue, green or violet girdles and wearing white caps have a dancing lesson during which they learned minuets and folk dances.

Within four years, the school had become one of the most sought after in London and was described as 'the young ladies' Eton'. Although the girls learned English, geography, history and French, they were expected to spend much of their time learning social graces and being trained extensively in manners, decorum, how to enter and leave a room, and how to sit and rise correctly. They had to practise entering and leaving coaches, greeting people, paying calls and receiving visitors, and writing numerous letters.

From 1785-86 Jane and her sister Cassandra spent a year as parlour boarders at The Abbey School, Reading, which was a school for daughters of the clergy and minor gentry. Their father paid the school £37 19s per girl every six months to cover their board, tuition, needlework, French, washing materials and dancing lessons. They also learned to play the piano, gained some social skills and took part in plays. Towards the end of the year, their father's lack of money meant they stopped being parlour boarders and joined the rest of the school for meals.

Mary Somerville experienced a very different education when she was sent to a Scottish school in the early 1790s. She recalled:

> At ten years old I was sent to a boarding school kept by Miss Primrose at Musselburgh, where I was utterly wretched. The chief thing I had to do was to learn by heart a page of Johnson's

> Dictionary, not only to spell the words, give their parts of speech and meaning, but as an exercise of memory to remember their order of succession. Besides I had to learn the first principles of writing, and the rudiments of French and English grammar. The method of teaching was extremely tedious and inefficient. Our religious duties were attended in a remarkable way. Some of the girls were Presbyterians, others belonged to the Church of England, so Miss Primrose cut the matter short by taking us all to the kirk in the morning and the church in the afternoon.

In 1798, Mary Russell Mitford learned French, history, geography, music, drawing, dancing and needlework at the St Quinn's school in Hans Place, Chelsea. An unusual extra subject – for girls at least – was Latin. Her father disagreed with this, telling her 'your mother and I have had much conversation regarding the utility of your learning Latin, and we both agree it is perfectly unnecessary and would occasion you additional trouble.'

Around the same time, Susan Sibbald attended a school kept by the Misses Lea at Belevedere House, Bath where she was taught needlework, dancing, a little French and geography:

> [There was] no want of good living … generally roast beef on Mondays, on Tuesdays and Fridays roast shoulders of mutton, a round of beef on Wednesdays, Thursdays boiled legs of mutton, stewed beef and pickled walnuts on Saturdays. Then two days of the week we had 'choke dogs' dumplings with currants, other days rice or other puddings … A few of the girls remained a few minutes after the others had gone up to the school room and had a glass of port wine each, for which an extra charge was made.

Life at school could also be dangerous, resulting in serious illnesses with parents rarely being informed. Girls were generally left to recover as best they could. Living at close quarters, sharing beds, a lack of cleanliness and hygiene meant that diseases quickly spread.

This is well illustrated by Jane's early school experience. Aged 7 and 10 years old respectively, Jane and Cassandra Austen, along with their cousin Jane Cooper, were sent to a boarding school in Oxford, run by a Mrs Cawley. Within a few months, a measles outbreak led to the school being moved rapidly to Southampton, where the girls caught typhoid. Mrs Cawley did not inform their parents, who only discovered what had happened when Jane Cooper sent a letter to her parents in Bath. This prompted their respective parents to quickly remove the children from Mrs Crawley's school.

Ill health caused by a boarding school environment was also encountered by Bobbin, the youngest daughter of agriculturalist Arthur Young. In 1791, he sent his daughter to Campden House in Chelsea. He quickly regretted it, writing in his journal that:

> the rules of health are detestable, no air but one measured formal walk, and all running and quick motions prohibited. Preposterous! She slept with a girl who could hear only with one ear, and so ever laid on one side, and my dear girl could not otherwise without pain, because the vile beds are so small that they must both lie the same way. The school discipline of all sorts, the food … all contributed. She never had a bellyful of breakfast … How I regret ever putting her, or to any other, for they are all theatres of knavery, liberality and infamy. Upon her being ill in March, I took her away to my lodgings in Jermyn Street, where Dr Turton attended her until April 12 when I carried her to Bradfield.

Bobbin died soon afterwards, and it has been suggested by some that she had caught tuberculosis.

Such experiences were not unusual. In 1809, J.L. Chirol's *Enquiry into the Best System of Female Education* reported that there were schools where the bed linen was 'scarcely changed oftener than every four or five months'. He went on to note that girls were not very clean, washed hands and faces and combed hair but that 'other extremities which are more exposed to dirt, are washed only once in six weeks or two months, and the body never, not even in summer.'

In 1818, aged just 3 years old, Elizabeth Sewell was sent to Miss Crookes' school on the Isle of Wight. Later recalling her experience, she remembered:

> the wretchedness of the large bedroom, the two blocked up windows, with a third we were forbidden to even to look out of, on pain of paying half a crown; the great worm-eaten four post bedsteads, without an atom of curtain or drapery, the deal tables for washing stands with the jugs holding rainwater in which wonderful specimens of entomology disported themselves ... the touch of the coarse sheets ... and the sight of the large horn lanthorn, put upon the floor in the centre of the room, as our only light whilst undressing, were as chilling and depressing to the mind as to the body. In this large room we used to sit in the winter mornings learning our lessons until we were called down to a breakfast of milk and water, with an allowance of three pieces of thick bread and butter.

Further north, in Yorkshire, the Bronte sisters – Maria, Elizabeth, Charlotte and Emily – were sent to the Cowan Bridge School in 1824. Set up as a charitable school for the daughters of clergy, it was designed to equip them with the skills needed to be governesses or teachers. Poor hygiene and food, accompanied by a harsh lifestyle, soon created problems. There was an outbreak of typhoid fever leading to deaths among the pupils. Maria and Elizabeth were both sent home and died soon after of tuberculosis.

Writing in *Willingly to School*, Mary Cathcart Borer noted:

> There are countless authenticated stories of girls' boarding schools of the early nineteenth century when the education was useless and the conditions of living infinitely worse – schools with insufficient heating, where the food was totally inadequate, the bedrooms dirty and the bed-linen seldom changed, where girls had to sleep two or more to a bed and seldom had any proper exercise or fresh air.

Girls were taught posture from a very early age. They were expected to move with 'grace and ease', always keeping their backs straight, whether sitting or standing. In order to ensure they adopted the correct posture, girls often had to wear a backboard; a single piece of wood placed across the back and fastened with leather straps to keep it in place. This prevented slumping or sitting in any other way than totally upright.

Alongside education, changing fashions also created another hazard for young girls. Females were expected to have a fashionable shape, such as a long line for Empire line dresses, or a shaped waist for late Georgian style dresses. Wearing a corset, or stays, enabled the body shape to be adjusted as required. Fashion could even make an impact on the cost of food, as *Berrow's Worcester Journal* reported during a rise in food prices in 1767:

> We hear that the mistresses of several boarding schools, having taken into consideration the present high rate of Provisions, are come to a resolution to oblige the young ladies to take in their stays, in order that their stomachs may be laced so to accommodate them to the present artificial death.

Fashions changed dramatically during the late Georgian and Regency periods. Until the turn of the century, Georgian fashion meant small waists, with straight backs, and bell-shaped skirts. This required girls to wear a corset laced at the back, with carved wood or bone pieces stiffening the front from hips to bust. Tighter lacing at the waist created the impression of a smaller waist. Change came with the arrival of the neoclassical, Empire line styles from the late 1790s and early 1800s. These dresses were inspired by classical Greek and Roman statuary. Waistlines were high, located under the breasts, enabling the skirt to hang free in a columnar style while breasts were pushed upwards.

To achieve this desired effect, changes were made to corset styles. It marked the arrival of stays; a shorter corset which involved a combination of straps, tapes and lacing. Stiffened with cording and light boning, it allowed the outer garment to lie flat against the body while lifting and separating the breasts. A slightly longer form of stays adjusted the stomach to hips area, as well as the ribs and bust. It was claimed that not only did the stays create a desired body shape, but also improved posture. When wearing these stays, a lady was unable to slouch or bend freely at the waist.

Mary Somerville described her experience encountering stays for the first time as a 10-year-old at Miss Primrose's school in Musselburgh:

> A few days after my arrival, although perfectly straight and well made, I was enclosed in stiff stays with a steel busk in front, while above my frock, bands drew my shoulders back until my shoulder-blades met. Then a steel rod, with a semi-circle which went under the chin, was clasped to the steel busk in my stays. In this constrained state, I and most of the younger girls, had to prepare our lessons.

Once laced into their stays, it was not unknown for girls to have wear them for long periods – including sleeping in them. Girls often fainted due to lacing being too tight since it constricted their breathing, and also their digestion. They became reluctant to eat, encouraging the general belief that girls were delicate; a desirable feature since girls of breeding were not expected to feel hungry.

An additional underwear hazard for fashionable women appeared in 1806 with the arrival of drawers. Until this point, women, as illustrated in numerous cartoons created by Thomas Rowlandson, wore no such undergarments. The new drawers were basically a version of male breeches, tied at the waist with string and split in the middle creating two tubes of cloth. Described as popular with young girls, including Princess Charlotte, Augusta of Wales and the Duchess of Kent, some women experienced unhappy experiences, with one woman noting:

> They are the ugliest things I ever saw: I will never put them on again. I dragged my dress in the dirt for fear someone would spy them. My finest dimity pair with real Swiss lace is quite useless to me for I lost one leg and did not deem it proper to pick it up, and so walked off leaving it in the street behind me, and the lace had cost six shillings a yard.

In 1810, James Gillray satirised the practice of using stays to create a fashionable shape in a series of images known as 'Progress of the Toilet'. An image entitled 'The Stays' shows a woman being tightly laced into an uncomfortable whalebone corset so as to achieve the socially acceptable female shape. She is also wearing drawers, caught tightly at the knee.

Achieving a fashionable shape was regarded as extremely important to women, especially if they were seeking a husband. Written by an unnamed Lady of Distinction in 1811, *The Mirror of Graces* highlighted aspects of etiquette, dress and manners of ladies during the Regency period. She pointed out that a woman's appearance was a reflection of her character and that by dressing well, being graceful and accomplished, it would help a woman attract a suitor. The author advised that there were three key elements women should follow to preserve 'Beauty, Health and Loveliness' – temperance (moderation in eating and drinking), exercise and cleanliness. Turning to the subject of stays, she writes:

> to maintain the ease and gracefulness of our assumed Grecian mode, against a new race of stay-makers, corset inventors &c who have just armed themselves with whalebone, steel and buckram, to the utter destruction of all the naturally-elegant shapes which fall into their hands … in eight women out of ten, the hips squeezed into a circumference little more than the waist; and the bosom shoved up to the chin.

Much depended on the amount of lacing. As a result, when writing on the 'Duties of a Ladies Maid' in *The Mirror of Graces*, the anonymous Lady of Distinction noted, 'corsets may be made only harmless, but beneficial, if they are contrived so as to aid the muscles in support of the body. If they do more than this and are made to compress the chest and stomach by tight lacing, they become hurtful and destructive.'

Two years later, in 1813, Jane Austen wrote to her sister Cassandra in September noting how quickly fashion was changing. 'I learnt from Mrs Tickar's young Lady, to my high amusement, that the stays now are not made to force the Bosom up at all; - that was a very unbecoming, unnatural fashion. I was really glad to hear that they are not to be so much off the shoulders as they were.'

By the start of the 1820s, fashion had begun to move back towards lower waist-defining costumes. This resulted in demand for tighter waist and stomach lacing. Writing in *The Perfect Lady*, Dr Willett Cunningham noted a tradesman reported in 1820 that when one girl stooped down 'her stays gave way with a tremendous explosion and she fell to the ground. I thought she had snapped in two.'

Women had to be very careful when it came to clothing and behaviour. Showing any element of undergarment was deemed improper, as was too much exercise. In *Pride and Prejudice*, Elizabeth Bennet is accused of impropriety when she arrives at Netherfield to seek news of her ill sister. Instead of riding or taking a coach, Elizabeth had decided to walk across the fields. She arrives with 'weary ankles, dirty stockings, and a face glowing with the warmth of exercise'. Mr Darcy does not appear to mind this, but Miss Bingley and Mrs Hurst are extremely critical of her behaviour because of its 'conceited independence' and the fact that she displayed her petticoat:

> 'Very nonsensical to come at all! Why must *she* be scampering about the country, because her sister had a cold? Her hair so untidy, so blowsy!'
>
> 'Yes, and her petticoat; I hope you saw her petticoat, six inches deep in mud, I am absolutely certain; and the gown which had been let down to hide it, not doing its office.'

Chapter 3

The Marriage Mart

Marriage was the normal fate for almost every girl in this period; whatever their rank in society, they were expected to marry. In *Pride and Prejudice*, Charlotte Lucas' opinions on the matter are made clear:

> Without thinking highly either of men or of matrimony, marriage had always been her object; it was the only honourable provision for well-educated young women of small fortune, and, however uncertain of giving happiness, must be their pleasantest preservative from want.

Girls 'came out' in society at around 15 or 16 years of age. This was when they were officially introduced into adult society and expected to attract a husband; they had officially joined the marriage market. The process was very carefully managed by parents or guardians since girls needed to meet potential suitors and make good connections which would benefit themselves and their family. Social connections were all important. Acquiring the right connections through marriage meant rising in social status, which is why in *Pride and Prejudice*, Mrs Bennet is focused on ensuring her daughters make good marriages.

In *The Season: A Social History of the Debutante* Kirsten Richardson notes that marriage 'was the only means of advancement and the most secure way to live … It was nearly impossible for a woman to make an advantageous marriage if she did not have some combination of competitive dowry, exceptional beauty and perfect lineage.'

The chances of finding a suitable husband partly depended on a girl's status in society. Some marriages were pre-arranged. On hearing that she had become engaged to the heir to the Earl of Bessborough, Harriet Spencer, daughter of Lord Spencer said, 'I had not the least guess about it till the day papa told me. I wish I could have known him a little better first, but my dear papa and mama say it will make them the happiest of creatures ... I have a better chance of being reasonably happy with him than with most people I know.'

Most aristocratic and wealthy families aimed to launch a girl into London society since, as Kirsten Richardson points out, 'The only respectable career for women was marriage, and the best marriages were made by debutantes.'

As debutantes, girls from the aristocracy and upper gentry would be given a season in London. Sometimes girls from lower-class gentry families were invited to take part, usually as a companion to a more aristocratic friend or because of the kindness of an aristocratic relative. Coming out was expensive exercise involving the buying of lots of new clothes, some of which, such as the Presentation dress, might only be worn once. Most girls would only have one opportunity to make an impact and find a husband. Time was short. Lasting just twelve weeks, starting around May and ending in mid-August, the London Season became the centre of social life in the latter part of the eighteenth century.

'It became the place where marriages could be negotiated. A stream of rich young girls poured into the capital and began to coalesce into the first debutante scene, where there were multiple parties designed to make marriages take place over a period of months,' comments Kirsten Richardson.

The pre-eminent status of London as the centre of the debutante scene was emphasised when a group of aristocratic women set up

Almack's Assembly Room. They had found that relying on private balls to produce enough eligible bachelors did not work, and so by combining their efforts and making the Assembly balls an essential element in the marriage mart, they could consequently control the attendance. Its function was clearly recognisable. Grantley Berkeley, son of the Earl of Berkeley, described Almack's as being:

> one of the matrimonial marts of my time ... an institution that seemed expressly designed as the slave market at Aleppo for the appreciation and transfer of female attraction ... With the title of Lady Patronesses, they issued tickets for a series of balls for the gratification of the crème de la crème of society, with a jealous watchfulness to prevent the intrusion of plebeian rich or untitled vulgar, and they drew up a code of laws for the elect who received invitations, which were as unalterable as those of the Medes and Persians.

These patronesses not only organised the subscription fees but controlled the list of those invited to attend, thus gaining considerable social standing. People had to apply for vouchers before the Season started. The seven patronesses met each week to study the applications from relatives, friends and close connections, who were then either accepted or rejected. If rejected there were two options – those never to be admitted, and those who could apply again. Only 2,000 subscriptions were available in each season. Writing in *The Season*, Kirsten Richardson notes there was a contemporary report from an unnamed person indicating that:

> so anxious are the Committee of Almack's to promote matrimonial matches, that they often refuse to admit a young gentleman whom they think in marriageable circumstances, to a third season because he has 'done no good' in the two first. They

> reason this way; the young gentleman who in circumstances to justify his marrying, and who has withstood the female attractions of two seasons will, in all probability, become a confirmed bachelor.

An ability to dance well was a key element in gaining admittance to Almack's or indeed any social event. Dancing provided a way for both men and women to socialise in an acceptable fashion. The minuet was a stylistic dance involving just a handful of couples showing off their steps; quadrilles and country dances could be vigorous and allowed time for brief chats with partners; while the introduction of the waltz in 1813 aroused considerable concern, until it was made respectable by the endorsement of Countess Lieven, one of the Committee members of Almack's. Dancing masters taught the latest dances, and books such as *The Companion to the Ballroom* taught readers how to behave properly, along with the appropriate etiquette.

At the Netherfield Ball, Elizabeth has no choice but to dance with Mr Collins. If she had turned down his request, then she would not have been able to accept any other partners all evening. For Elizabeth, these dances become 'dances of mortification' since Mr Collins 'often moving wrong without being aware of it' provides 'all the shame and misery which a disagreeable partner for a couple of dances can give.'

Taking part in the Season became an exhausting experience for girls who were constantly aware of the limited time they had to attract a male. Debutantes experienced a non-stop round of social activities, balls, routs, concerts, private parties, dinners, sporting events and visits enabling them to meet other aristocrats and be presented at Court. Girls were presented in order of their father's rank and wore a dress that had to meet strict specifications, such as the number of feathers to be worn in the hair. Protocol was equally strict. Writing in 1785, Fanny Burney, lady in waiting to Queen Charlotte, indicated that girls should 'choke rather than cough, hold one's breath or break a blood vessel rather than sneeze. If a hair pin should prove painful, it was not to be removed.'

Attending balls could be extremely daunting. Rooms were crowded and became extremely hot thanks to the numerous candles used for lighting. In 1811, a ball was held to mark the beginning of the Prince of Wales' official regency on behalf of his father. The crush was said to be so great that ladies fainted, lost their shoes and even had their clothes torn off. Balls generally lasted for six hours or more, ending only as dawn approached. In *Sense and Sensibility*, Marianne is thrilled to hear that Willoughby danced 'from eight o'clock till four, without once sitting down.'

Clergymen's daughters, lower gentry and the daughters of professional people such as lawyers, experienced a quieter and less expensive introduction of the social round on reaching marriageable age. Regional versions of the Season appeared in places like Bath and Tunbridge Wells as well as greater focus on social activities in towns and cities around the country. Girls would attend local balls, dances, concerts, private parties, dinners and pay visits, accompanied by their mothers or a chaperone. Following the success of the assembly rooms in London, similar projects appeared nationwide, with buildings being built specifically for the purpose of holding balls on a weekly or bi-weekly basis. By 1820, seventy assembly rooms existed around England and Wales. Unlike the London Assembly Rooms, these regional ones involved purchasing a ticket, which could be bought by anyone who could afford it. In *Pride and Prejudice*, Caroline Bingley found it extremely embarrassing to be expected to attend a local Assembly where she might have to socially encounter the daughters of shopkeepers.

Women were also expected to fit the requirements of society and possess desirable qualities. Women were expected to be courteous, dignified, polite, gentle, meek and modest, and devoted to their family. They were not expected to be argumentative, although Thomas

Gisborne's *An Enquiry into the Duties of the Female Sex* believed that conversations should include 'laughter, wit and gaity' as well as serious topics. Flattering, flirting and the encouragement of vanity was not recommended.

Women had to be accomplished. According to Miss Bingley in *Pride and Prejudice*:

> A woman must have a thorough knowledge of music, singing, drawing, dancing, and the modern languages, to deserve the word; and besides all this, she must possess a certain something in her air and manner of walking, the tone of her voice, her address and expressions, or the word will be but half-deserved.

To which Mr Darcy adds, 'to all this she must yet add something more substantial, in the improvement of her mind by extensive reading.'

'To be witty was a flaw' as Lucy Worsley points out in her book *Jane Austen at Home*. *The Lady's Magazine* contained a letter from an unnamed Georgian lady complaining that if a woman 'dare to ready anything of more importance than a play or a novel, we are called critics, wits, female pedants.' Brash and over emotional women were not encouraged. Even laughing had to be undertaken quietly.

Women frequently indulged in 'the vapours' or fainting when under stress, upset or even encountering bad manners. Mrs Bennett in *Pride and Prejudice* frequently experiences an attack of the vapours or faints at the slightest episode. This is especially noticeable when news of Lydia's elopement arrives at Longbourne. It should be said, however, that tight fitting corsets did make women more susceptible to fainting.

Appropriate behaviour had to be constantly maintained. This governed the way in which females had to conduct themselves in society. When outside the house, they could not just stand and talk to a friend – they had to walk and talk. It was regarded as bad manners to ignore people, every acquaintance had to be acknowledged. They could not start a conversation with a person they had never met before – instead etiquette required that they must be officially introduced. Men had to take the lead when it came to introductions. This is seen very clearly in *Pride and Prejudice*, where Mr Bennett calls on the Bingleys first, otherwise the two households could not have interacted.

Women were not expected to be alone with a gentleman, especially if they were under the age of 30 and unmarried. A chaperone always had to be present, even when walking within a town, although this practice did slowly begin to change during Jane Austen's life, as women were gradually able to walk to church on their own or go out for an early morning walk.

The social round could be further upset by unexpected deaths putting a household into mourning. The length of the mourning period varied. Ladies had to stay in full mourning for twelve months after their husband died. The death of a parent or parent-in-law led to six months' mourning, and three months for the death of a sister, brother, aunt or uncle. During full mourning, ladies had to wear black and could not take part in society events. Towards the end of the mourning period, ladies could transition to half mourning and wear grey or lilac, and attend some society activities. They could go to a dance, but not actually dance until the full mourning period was complete.

Even at a ball, women had to take care to maintain their reputation. One dance with a partner was expected. Two dances indicated that a gentleman may be interested, but three dances with the same partner was unheard of. At assemblies, for example, the master of ceremonies would deliberately introduce women to a prospective dance partner. During dinner parties, ladies were expected to toy with their food and eat only small amounts since large appetites were regarded as unladylike. In *Sense and Sensibility*, Austen highlights the risks of spending too much time with one person when Marianne and Willoughby 'were partners for half the time; and when obliged to separate for a couple of dances, were careful to stand together and scarcely spoke a word to anybody else. Such conduct made them of course most exceedingly laughed at.'

Once Jane Austen reached a marriageable age, she was frequently sent away from home to visit relatives in Godmersham, Southampton, Bath and Gloucestershire. She had no choice in the matter. The arrangements were made and she was told where to go, where to stay and how she was to get there. During her stay at each location, it was up to her to take every advantage she could and meet as many eligible men as possible.

Travelling had to be undertaken under the protection of a male relation. In *Pride and Prejudice*, Sir William Lucas escorts his younger daughter Maria and Elizabeth to stay with the newly married Charlotte Collins (formerly Charlotte Lucas). Travel tended to be slow and tiring. Using your own horses and carriage meant that the horses had to be rested frequently along the way, whereas hiring a post-chaise meant that horses were simply replaced every 10 to 15 miles. Gentlewomen like Jane Austen did not travel by stagecoach unless there was no other option available. Overnight stays at inns could be uncomfortable, with damp beds and a general lack of cleanliness. Luggage often went missing en route. Travelling to Kent, Jane discovered that her writing and dressing boxes had accidently been put on a chaise for Gravesend and onwards to the West Indies – they were rescued just in time.

Her visit to Bath in 1797 provided an opportunity to take part in the Bath marriage mart. Her wealthy aunt and uncle Jane and James Leigh-Perrot had rented a house for the Season, at No 1 The Paragon. The daily programme involved a morning walk to the Pump Room, where her uncle would drink the waters and they would meet acquaintances. Shopping in the fashionable Milsom Street might follow, or a visit to exhibitions, the library or even a stroll through Sydney Gardens or along the banks of the river Avon. Such locations were places where marriageable girls could see and be seen by society. Sometimes there would be a trip to a local beauty spot, preferably with a suitor.

After dinner, people would visit the theatre or the assembly rooms to enjoy dancing and cards. There was a strict ranking for seating, organised by the Master of Ceremonies. The first bench was for girls on the marriage market, and this was where Jane Austen sat in 1797. The second bench was for older ladies.

The search for suitors continued even after the Reverend Austen retired. Living in Bath, the girls had access to the social activities in places like the assembly rooms. They also went on countless visits to relatives. In 1802, the Austens toured Dawlish, Teignmouth and visited Tenby in South Wales. The following year there were trips to Lyme Regis, Charmouth and Uplyme in Dorset, as well as Ramsgate in Kent. Cassandra noted that at one such location, her sister Jane met a gentleman thought to be a doctor or clergyman who expressed great interest and hoped to see them again. There is no record as to whether this ever happened.

Marriage was essential within the landed classes, wealthy merchants and lawyers since it was the only way in which a legal heir could be provided to ensure the continuation of a family and estate. For women, it was quite simply the sole reason for their existence. A women's education, upbringing and social activities were all geared towards the prospect of finding a suitable husband and becoming a wife and mother.

In Jane Austen's novels, marriage is presented as the best option and the ideal solution for girls. Emma Woodhouse marries Mr Knightley, Jane and Elizabeth Bennet wed Mr Bingley and Mr Darcy, Fanny Price marries Edmund Bertram, while Anne Elliot (finally) marries Captain Wentworth. Despite her Gothic horror experiences, Catherine Morland eventually finds true love at the altar with Henry Tilney, and marrying Edward Ferrars and Colonel Brandon rescues the Dashwood sisters Elinor and Marianne from loneliness and poverty.

Mothers had the duty of ensuring their daughters were well married so as to ensure their financial wellbeing, while unmarried men needed a wife to secure family and property. This is clearly stressed in *Pride and Prejudice* with the famous opening lines, 'It is a truth universally acknowledged, that a single man in possession of a good fortune, must be in want of a wife.'

Eligible men were immediately targeted by mothers keen to find a husband for their daughters, which is why Mrs Bennet gleefully tells her husband that Mr Bingley has taken up residence in Netherfield:

> 'A single man of large fortune, four or five thousand a year. What a fine thing for our girls!'

> '... consider your daughters. Only think what an establishment it would be for one of them. Sir William and Lady Lucas are determined to go, merely on that account; for in general, you know, they visit no newcomers. Indeed you must go, for it will be impossible for *us* to visit him if you do not.'

Men were expected to announce their intentions within a few occasions of paying attention at social events and visiting a young woman's home.

It was unusual for a woman to turn down a suitor, as her consent was generally taken for granted. To reject a suitor could well mean that the young lady might not encounter anyone else prepared to marry her – the availability of potential suitors was often quite small in number. Most women encountered only one suitor and were pressurised to agree on the basis that no other suitor might appear, as Mr Collins points out to Elizabeth:

> ... you should take it into further consideration that, in spite of your manifold attractions, it is by no means certain that another offer of marriage may ever be made you. Your portion is unhappily so small, that it will in all likelihood undo the effects of your loveliness and amiable qualifications.

Even if rejected, this was often seen as being the prequel to eventual consent, as Mr Collins intimates in his proposal: '...it is usual with young ladies to reject the addresses of the man whom they secretly mean to accept, when he first applies for their favour ... I am, therefore, by no means discouraged by what you have just said, and shall hope to lead you to the altar ere long.'

Even when Elizabeth stresses that she remains 'perfectly serious' in her refusal, Mr Collins remains undaunted: 'your refusal of my addresses are merely words, of course ... you are not serious in your rejection of me.'

Young women could come under severe pressure to agree to a marriage, even if they were opposed to it. Determined to get a daughter married to someone she regards as suitable, Mrs Bennet tells Mr Collins that '... Lizzy shall be brought to reason. I will speak to her about it myself directly. She is a very headstrong foolish girl, and does not know her own interest; but I will *make* her know it.' She even invokes Mr Bennet's support telling him that 'You must come and make Lizzy marry Mr Collins, for she vows she will not have him.'

Love rarely came into the equation. Indeed, the majority of single women would have fully appreciated the reality behind Charlotte Lucas' comment to her friend Elizabeth after she accepts Mr Collin's proposal of marriage instead:

> I am not romantic, you know. I never was. I ask only a comfortable home; and, considering Mr Collins' character, connections, and situation in life, I am convinced that my chance of happiness

> with him is as fair as most people can boast on entering the marriage state.

Charlotte was quick to recognise an opportunity as soon as she discovered that Elizabeth had rejected Mr Collins by immediately spending time with him and inviting him to visit. Mr Collins is equally quick to react. At 27 years old, with no money and no prospects, Charlotte desperately wants a home and security.

The engagement of Charlotte and Mr Collins is welcomed by her family; especially her younger sisters and brothers, whose future plans were immediately changed as a result: 'Younger girls formed hopes of coming out a year or two sooner than they might otherwise have done; and the boys were relieved from their apprehension of Charlotte's dying an old maid.'

Once accepted, an engagement almost inevitably led to a wedding, although there were a few occasional exceptions. It was not unknown for difficulties in negotiating a marriage settlement to result in the ending of an engagement, and sometimes the woman changed her mind. In 1802, Jane Austen received a proposal from Harris Bigg-Wither. He was a regarded as a desirable suitor, being the heir to a country house and property to the value of £20,000 per annum. Jane and Cassandra had long been friends with his sisters and marrying him would mean that Jane could return to live in the Hampshire countryside she loved. But there was a downside. Harris Bigg-Wither was five years her junior and has been described as unprepossessing. After giving her consent, she revoked it the day afterwards and immediately fled the house with her sister to seek refuge at her brother's rectory.

Some years later, Jane's niece Anna Austen broke off her engagement to Michael Terry, the rector of Dummer. It had been a match made in the face of her parents' opposition. He was twice her age and was referred to locally as 'poor blundering Michael Terry', while other contemporary accounts described him as being 'tall and good looking and well connected with the certainty of a comfortable family living in Hampshire'.

Heiresses were much sought after, especially by younger sons without property of their own. In Henry Fielding's novel *Tom Jones*, (1749) Sophia's status as the sole heiress to her father's fortune means there is considerable competition for her hand in marriage. Her family ignore her personal love interest – Tom Jones – because he is of a lower social class and insist instead on her marriage to the person they choose.

Under the terms of the 1753 Marriage Act, girls under 21 years of age needed the permission of parents to marry. If such permission could not be obtained, a wealthy couple could obtain a special license from the Archbishop of Canterbury. Such a license was expensive and so eloping to Gretna Green was regarded as the most viable, although risky, option. Gretna Green was the first town after crossing the Scottish border, and as getting married in Scotland did not require the services of a clergyman, all the eloping couple needed were witnesses to their promise to cohabit as a married couple.

Angry relatives often pursued an eloping couple and, given the poor road conditions at the time, often stood a good chance of catching them. The route to Gretna Green was not an easy one, and it was approximately 320 miles from London. According to Cary's *New Itinerary: Or An Accurate Delineation of the Great Roads* written in 1798, the usual route was via the Great North Road, turning westwards at Manchester, and then following turnpike roads up the western side of the country before crossing the border and reaching Gretna Green. Since the average carriage travelled at around 7 miles an hour, and taking into account the need to pay tolls, change horses and the inevitable delays due to road and weather conditions, the journey could take five days or more. It was also a costly journey. Hiring a carriage could cost around 1 and 3 pence per mile, giving a total cost of £20 – at a time when a housemaid earned at most £16 a year. In addition, the eloping couple would have to pay tolls and accommodation as well as the costs (and often bribes) of drivers and postilions. Once at Gretna Green, more payments had to be made to the person undertaking the task of uniting them in marriage, which might be a blacksmith, a fisherman or a joiner. The exact price paid for the service reflected information provided by the coachman, and might have been 2 guineas or more according to contemporary accounts.

The risk of being caught was always present. One such elopement was reported in the *Hampshire Chronicle* in 1809. A young lady by the name of Augusta Nicholson was due to inherit £14,000 when she came of age. She was a ward of chancery, living with her stepmother (referred to in the newspaper as her mother-in-law). During a visit to Tunbridge Wells, a fashionable spa town, Augusta met a young man named John Giles, who was a penniless comedian. He had apparently carried her library books home for her. A whirlwind romance ensued. According to the newspaper:

> On the following evening, she went to the theatre, accompanied by her mother-in-law; and sat on the front seat of the stage-box; and while Mr Giles was performing close to the box, Miss N. contrived to drop a letter to him unobserved, which he picked up, also unperceived by the mother-in-law. In that letter she acknowledged her attachment to him, and gave him encouragement to pay his addresses to her, and that she would marry him. From that time, a mutual intercourse and correspondence took place, in which the warmest affection was expressed – This proceeding was communicated to Miss N's mother-in-law, who to prevent the intercourse proceeding further, confined her to the house. This regulation, however, had not the desired effect; for Mr Giles contrived a plan for exchanging letters through the key-hole of the street door.

> Miss N. had a bedroom to herself, and got up every morning before five o'clock, and conversed with her lover out of the window. This correspondence continued about five weeks previous to the elopement.

The couple decided to elope. Needing cash to arrange the elopement, John Giles borrowed £30 from a fellow actor and hired a chaise and four. He took Augusta to London, purchased a wedding ring, and had the banns read twice at Marylebone church. Augusta made Giles swear on the Bible that he would never marry anyone else.

Before the marriage could finally take place, the Nicholson family solicitor tracked Augusta down. The *Hampshire Chronicle* noted that 'a frantic tragic scene took place … Both lovers rushed into each other's arms, and swore attachment, beating their heads, and running about the room distracted.'

Since Augusta was a ward of court, Giles was sent to Fleet Prison. Despite this situation, their relationship was maintained and in the spring of 1810, the duo were eventually married, but it did not end happily. Augusta gave birth to a little boy, but four days before she came of age in 1811, she died. Her brother inherited her share of the estate because, as she was underage, he was the only legal inheritor. The *Hampshire Chronicle* reported what happened next since the situation left 'father and infant under many pecuniary and unavoidable embarrassments'. Augusta's brother died suddenly and so by this 'immediate death, the infant becomes entitled to the whole of its mother's portion.'

A distant cousin of Jane Austen's through the Leigh family tree was also involved in an elopement. This was Margaret, the elder daughter of the wealthy William Beckford and Lady Margaret Gordon. Her mother had died giving birth to Margaret's younger sister Susan and the two girls had been well educated and were known for their beauty. Margaret caused considerable gossip and was eventually disowned by her father when she eloped in 1811 with James Orde, an Army colonel. The event caused Jane Austen to refer to the 'shocking elopement' of 'our cousin Margaret'. Margaret died in Bath just seven years later.

In *Pride and Prejudice*, Wickham tries to elope with Georgiana Darcy without her brother's knowledge in order to gain control of her fortune. He is only prevented from doing so when Darcy arrives unexpectedly and Georgiana confides in him. Likewise, in *Sanditon*, Sir Edward Denham models himself on Samuel Richardson's rakish character Lovelace, who abducts and rapes Clarissa Harlowe. As a result, Denham decides that '… he was formed to be a dangerous man – quite in the line of the Lovelaces ... it was Clara whom he meant to seduce. Her seduction was quite determined upon ... If she could not be won by affection, he must carry her off.' His aim was simple: 'ruin and disgrace for the object of his affections.'

The speed at which a wedding took place depended entirely on the husband's financial circumstances. If he could afford to keep a wife, and ultimately a family, then the wedding took place as soon as the marriage settlement had been organised. If insufficient money existed and everything depended on future prospects, particularly when it came to marrying a member of the clergy, then considerable time could pass between an engagement and the actual marriage service. Cassandra Austen became engaged to the Reverend Tom Fowle in 1792, but five years later, in 1797, Fowle was still seeking a suitable living to support a wife when he died on board a ship heading to the West Indies. Jane's naval officer brother, Frank Austen, met his future wife, Mary Gibson, in 1803, but they could not afford to marry until 1806.

Around 170,000 weddings took place annually and were invariably church weddings. As soon as a daughter was married, it was expected that she would help younger sisters to find a husband. In *Pride and Prejudice*, Jane and Elizabeth's younger sister Catherine (Kitty) regularly goes to stay with them after their respective marriages.

Such visits would enable the young lady to meet a much wider pool of suitors than would normally be possible from her father's home. Friends also expected to benefit from fortunate weddings and were always intent on maintaining visiting rights in order to meet potential suitors. In *Pride and Prejudice*, Caroline Bingley had always wanted to marry Mr Darcy but despite being 'deeply mortified' on hearing of Darcy's choice of Elizabeth as a bride, remains determined to 'retain the right of visiting' Pemberley due the scope it presents within the wider marriage market.

Chapter 4

After the Wedding

Once married, a woman became the responsibility of her husband, who was expected to maintain her status and position in society. He gained control of any assets, money and property. Occasionally, such access was limited by the decrees of trustees, as can be seen by the marriage of Jane's cousin Eliza Hancock and Army officer Jean-François Capot de Feuillide, who became a French count. The match met with considerable opposition from her trustees, including the Reverend Austen. Although the marriage went ahead and the couple moved to the south of France, Eliza returned to England when she became pregnant because her husband wanted the child to be known to the trustees and accepted as heir to her fortune. Eliza never went back to her husband, who was subsequently sent to the guillotine during the French Revolution. Since the Reverend Austen had not allowed Eliza's husband to invest her dowry in France, she still had her money and was careful with it, avoiding contracting debts or gambling.

Women had no legal rights on marriage and were regarded as being one unit with their husband. A woman could not enter into any contracts, had no say in where she lived, and could be forced to relocate against her wishes. She was expected to bear children and could be physically abused by her husband. If she tried to leave him, then he could legally prevent her from doing so. All children of the marriage had to remain with the husband, and the mother would not necessarily become their guardian in the event of the father's death, as the husband had the right to name someone else as their guardian.

Women could not be sued in Common Law without her husband, and this meant she could not sue her husband if he refused to maintain her. If that happened, then technically she could purchase items on credit, making him liable for the resulting debt; an option that was taken by increasing numbers of estranged wives during the eighteenth and nineteenth centuries.

The only positive right that a woman retained in marriage were her dower rights. If she outlived her husband, she had the right to a life interest in one third of her husband's freehold lands, as well as any dowry brought to the marriage through her marriage settlement, as indicated in Chapter 1. This situation persisted unchanged throughout much of the nineteenth century and it was not until the passing of the Married Women's Property Act in 1882 that married women could finally own their own property.

Even in the event of a marriage settlement, widows and daughters could still be left in difficult circumstances following the death of a husband and father, as can be seen from the experience of the Harwoods at Deane House; the location of the ball where Jane Austen danced with Tom Lefoy, a gentlemen often regarded as the man she would have liked to have married. On the death of his father, Mr Harwood had expected to inherit an estate of £1,200 a year, just as previous generations had done. Unknown to him or to any of his family, it turned out that the older Mr Harwood had 'borrowed and mortgaged' so freely that it left nothing for his widow and daughter. The son was 'a ruined man … blighted in all his hopes and prospects,' and his marriage plans impossible. He had hoped to marry a widow by the name of Mrs Heathcote (formerly known as Elizabeth Bigg-Wither) and a long-time friend of Jane Austen's. Soon after the marriage plans ended, Elizabeth encountered more problems after her father died. Her brother and his wife immediately asked her to leave Manydown House, and in 1814 Elizabeth went to live in Winchester.

Another example is that of Catherine Tylney-Long, an heiress who has been described as the richest commoner in Regency England. She married William Wellesley-Pole, who turned out to be a spendthrift, rapidly spending her inheritance. Eventually they had to sell the family home, and Catherine ended her life in poverty.

Once married, women had little option but to stay with their husband. Marriage was expected to be for life, even if they were miserable. In *Pride and Prejudice*, the marriage of Louisa Bingley and Mr Hurst is clearly unhappy. They have little in common and Mr Hurst is only interested in food and cards.

In *Decency and Disorder* Ben Wilson comments that:

> 'A woman is too often reduced to this dilemma,' muses Maria Edgeworth's Belinda. 'Either she must marry a man she does not love, or she must be blamed by the world – Either she must sacrifice a portion of her reputation, or the whole of her happiness.' Whatever the motives for banishing passion from marriage, the arrangement invariably meant unhappy marriages and every incentive to see pleasure elsewhere. It made rakes of men and coquettes of women. Forced into an unhappy marriage, couples 'think of nothing but how it may be palliated, and to alleviate their feelings, they solace themselves, one in the arms of a mistress, and the other in those of a gallant.'

If a wife was mistreated and abused, the marriage would continue. There was no choice. A woman would lose custody of children in the event of a separation or divorce. If a married man took a mistress, the wife could not seek divorce or claim damages. If an unhappy couple was determined to end the relationship, they were initially to seek a remedy via the Church courts. These courts offered two options:

- Annulment on the basis of a marriage being invalid due to an impediment such as incest at the time of marriage.
- Separation from bed and board.

Adultery, cruelty, bigamy, incest, sodomy were the key grounds for separation – but success depended on your sex. Men merely had to provide evidence of adultery, while women had to prove cruelty or other grounds as well.

However, even if a separation was granted, it did not dissolve the marriage. Under Common Law, the separated couples remained married. This meant that any money owned, inherited or earned by the woman still belonged to the husband. It was a situation that enabled vindictive husbands to effectively take money from an estranged wife, knowing that she could not take any action against him. He could also run up debts and be sued for them, using the resultant court orders to dispossess his wife of any assets since they belonged to him. Although the Church courts could order maintenance to be paid to a separated wife, it could not be enforced under Common Law, and required a third party – a man – to act on their behalf.

Obtaining a divorce was extremely difficult for a male, and virtually impossible for women. Until the Divorce Act of 1857, all divorces required an Act of Parliament – a measure that was prohibitively expensive. Since the husband controlled a woman's finances, women could not pay for legal action. In the event of a husband suing for divorce, and it being granted by Parliament, then Parliament would decide what happened to any money and land brought into the marriage by the marriage agreement. Potentially, a wife could lose everything.

Within high society, adultery was quite common. By far the most notorious of such relationships was that of Admiral Nelson and Emma Hamilton, while the Prince Regent was notorious as an energetic adulterer – a situation which did not endear him to Jane Austen, who supported the prince's wife, Caroline of Brunswick.

The Regency period is sometimes described as the 'Age of Scandal', especially relating to the activities of politicians, society hostesses and the Prince Regent's Carlton House crowd. There are numerous other examples, such as the Duke of Devonshire, who lived with his wife as well as his mistress Lady Elizabeth Foster, having children by both women and bringing them up as a group. The Prince Regent himself had numerous adulterous affairs, as well as undertaking a secret morganatic marriage to Maria Fitzherbert, a Roman Catholic widow, without his father's consent. He was forced to marry a woman he hated, Princess Caroline of Brunswick, and refused to let her take part in his coronation, even introducing a bill (later rescinded) to dissolve the marriage.

Lord Craven, a remote connection of Jane's friend Martha Lloyd, took a 15-year-old girl Harriette Wilson as his mistress. Harriette later became the mistress of the Duke of Wellington and wrote her memoirs recounting all the men she had known. As a young boy, the Earl of Portsmouth had been tutored at Steventon by the Reverend George Austen. Subsequently, Jane attended balls at the earl's home, Hurstbourne Park. Described as being of 'limited intelligence', the earl was married to Mary Anne Hansen in 1814. Mary Anne disliked her husband and treated him badly, even whipping him. Eventually, the earl was declared insane and Mary Anne married her live-in lover, William Rowland Alder, and had three children by him.

Adultery and divorce were very much part of Jane Austen's world. Within Jane's own extended family, Mary Cassandra Twistleton was one such divorcee. Following a visit to the Bath Assembly Rooms, Jane noted that she had seen her distant cousin, the notorious Mary Cassandra, writing 'I am proud to say I have had a very good eye at an Adulteress … A resemblance to Mrs Leigh was my guide. She is not so pretty as I expected: her face has the same defect as her sister's [Mrs Leigh].' The divorce had been a high-profile legal action which had included statements from her maid that Mary Cassandra had bragged about the sexual prowess of her lover, Charles William Taylor, the MP for Wells, compared to that of her husband Mr Rickets. Mary Cassandra's elder brother had also been involved in a messy divorce case. After forming an unsuitable relationship during amateur theatricals, her brother had eloped to Scotland, but the marriage turned out to be a disaster. He divorced his wife and became a clergyman, eventually taking on the position of Bishop of Colombo in order to escape the scandal.

The Paget family were well-known to the Austens, with Sir Charles Paget recommending Charles Austen for a naval command. It was a family which experienced considerable marital scandals. Sir Charles' brother, the Marquis of Anglesey, left his wife and eight children in 1808 and eloped with a married woman, Lady Charlotte Wellesley, the sister-in-law of the Duke of Wellington. As a result, both the marriages of the Marquis of Anglesey and that of Lady Charlotte Wellesley ended in notorious divorce proceedings. The marquis had to pay £24,000 damages to Charlotte's husband Henry Wellesley and fight a dual with her brother, Captain Cadogan. The marquis' divorced wife, Caroline Paget, then married her lover, the Duke of Argyll. Yet another member of the Paget family, Sir Arthur Paget, married Lady Boringdon in 1808 following her divorce in order to legitimise their child.

During that same year, another Austen family acquaintance was involved in a similar scandal. This involved Viscount Sackville and Lieutenant Colonel Thomas Powlett. While staying at the White Hart Inn, Winchester, Viscount Sackville was discovered in 'a compromising situation' with Mrs Mary Letitia Powlett. Jane Austen noted that 'this is such a sad story about Mrs Powlett. I should not have suspected her of such a thing. A hint of it, with initials, was in yesterday's *Courier*; and Mr Moore guessed it to be Ld Sackville, believing there was no other

Viscount S. in the peerage, and so it proved.' Although Lieutenant Colonel Powlett sought damages of £10,000, the court ordered that Lord Sackville should only pay £3,000.

Public humiliation could sometimes result from such scandals. In 1811, Lord Petersham was discovered in bed with Lady Frances Webster. Her husband chased Lord Petersham and horsewhipped him in the street. In *Mansfield Park*, Mr Price recommended similar action, commenting:

> I don't know what Sir Thomas may think of such matters; he may be too much of the courtier and fine gentleman to like his daughter the less. But by G–, if she belonged to *me*, I'd give her the rope's end as long as I could stand over her. A little flogging for man and woman too, would be the best way of preventing such things.

Examples of actual divorces taking place are few and far between in Jane Austen's novels. Mr Brandon divorces his wife for adultery in *Sense and Sensibility*, while in *Mansfield Park* the implications of a divorce are clearly outlined. It meant social disaster for the wife. Maria Bertram Rushworth has an adulterous relationship with Henry Crawford and as a result, her wealthy husband James Rushworth divorces her via an Act of Parliament. However, once the divorce is arranged, Crawford refuses to marry Maria and she has no claim against him for support. Her reputation was now in shreds:

> She hoped to marry him, and they continued together till she was obliged to be convinced that such hope was vain, and till the disappointment and wretchedness arising from the conviction rendered her temper so bad, and her feelings for him so like hatred, as to make them for a while each other's punishment, and then induce a voluntary separation.

Maria is left legally independent, but legally impoverished as she no longer has any place in society. Most people refuse to acknowledge her and her father, Sir Thomas Bertram, is appalled by her behaviour. It is only through moral obligation that he provides any help at all – and it means banishing her to stay with an elderly aunt in another country:

> Where she could be placed, became a subject of most melancholy and momentous consultation. Mrs Norris ... would have had her received at home and countenanced by them all. Sir Thomas would not hear of it ... As a daughter ... she should be protected by him, and secured in every comfort, and supported by every encouragement to do right ... but farther than *that*, he would not go. Maria had destroyed her own character.

It was not just divorce and separation that could destroy a woman's character. Unwise decisions with regard to suitors could result in very serious implications, both for the female involved and her family. The story of Lydia Bennet in *Pride and Prejudice* shows this clearly, as Elizabeth points out to Mr Darcy: 'My youngest sister has left all her friends – has eloped: has thrown herself into the power of – of Mr Wickham. They are gone off together from Brighton ... She has no money, no connections, nothing that can tempt him to – she is lost forever.' It soon becomes clear, however, that Wickham had no intention of marrying her and that they were living unmarried in London.

Eloping was bad enough, but taking part in pre-marital sex destroyed reputations. As Mary Bennet states, 'the loss of virtue in a female is irretrievable – that one false step involves her in endless ruin.'

Jane and Elizabeth Bennet knew that Lydia's actions will affect everyone in the family – especially her sisters. Almost immediately on hearing the news, Elizabeth realises that 'every thing *must* sink under such a proof of family weakness, such an assurance of the deepest disgrace'. Their chances of finding suitable husbands – especially in the forms of Mr Bingley and Mr Darcy – are now in ruins. This belief is reinforced when Mr Collins writes to tell them:

> … you are grievously to be pitied, in which opinion I am not only joined by Mrs Collins, but likewise by Lady Catherine and her daughter ... They agree with me in apprehending that this false step in one daughter will be injurious to the fortunes of all the others; for who, as Lady Catherine herself condescendingly says, will connect themselves with such a family?

Lydia regains some element of a reputation for herself and her sisters after eventually marrying Wickham, but this is only achieved after Wickham is 'worked on' and bribed by Mr Darcy. She has to go and live with her aunt and uncle Gardiner until the marriage can be arranged in London, before the duo can be sent as far away as possible so as to minimize the harm that has resulted from her carelessness.

It was not just the damage to reputations that was at stake in such situations. The risk of pregnancy was always present. Contraception was difficult and was a subject women would have had no information about. Most women would know little about sexual intercourse, or how babies were created before the wedding night, when the mother might give some vague explanation. In *Sense and Sensibility*, the relationship between Eliza Williams and John Willoughby results in an unplanned pregnancy and Eliza's own ruin: 'He had left the girl whose youth and innocence he had seduced, in a situation of the utmost distress, with no creditable home, no help, no friends, ignorant of his address!'

If traced, the authorities could have forced Willoughby to provide support for the child, but Eliza had no such expectation of support being provided for herself. It is left to Colonel Brandon to provide some help and support. He later remarks that 'she left to my care her only child, a little girl, the offspring of her first guilty connection, who was then about three years old.'

Another example of the problems facing an unwed mother is that of Agnes in Charles Dickens', *Oliver Twist*. Agnes Fleming, a gently born woman, had been engaged to Oliver's father Edwin Leeford, a rich man. Unfortunately, Edwin died before the marriage could take place, leaving Agnes pregnant and alone. She eventually seeks refuge in a workhouse, where she gives birth and dies in childbirth. It is only after considerable time that Oliver's real identity is discovered and he is returned to his mother's family. Although written twenty years after Jane's death, the attitudes expressed in *Oliver Twist* had changed very little in the intervening years.

The fate of children born as a result of such situations could be equally dire. Regarded as bastards, they could not inherit and had no rights at all. If they were destitute, then the requirements of the Poor Laws required the overseers of their local parish to provide support. The overseers could seek out the child's parents to demand that financial support be provided by the father, or could insist on his imprisonment. It was not unknown for overseers to force a couple into marriage as a way of removing their child from parish care.

Successfully finding and forcing a man to provide support for an illegitimate child meant that the funds were given to the mother to ensure the child's care. However, it was not unknown for some concern to be expressed that women of immoral habits could collect a number of such payments from various men in respect of a train of bastards, until she became a local heiress and could make an advantageous match.

Once married, women also had no say as to where they might live, the use of their income or the number of pregnancies. A wife could be physically abused by her husband and prevented from leaving. In general, couples lived together as best they could, in most cases enjoying genuine companionship if not love, as shown by the example of Charlotte Lucas and Mr Collins.

Intriguingly, the views and attitudes on marriage given in Jane Austen's novels led them to be forbidden reading in some nineteenth century girls' schools within the southern states of the USA. Kristen Richardson, author of *The Season: A Social History of the Debutante* notes that books by Sir Walter Scott and other chivalrous authors were allowed but

> girls schools limited which other novels girls could read, particularly novels that questioned courtship and marriage conventions. In an Augusta, Georgia girls' school, Jane Austen and the Bronte sisters were kept under lock and key until as late as 1890, and girls could read these novels only with permission and after the school day was finished. The stories of Scott exalted a world that was simple and pure and where good and evil were obvious.

Chapter 5

The Fishing Fleet to India

Women unable to find a husband, for whatever reason, within the ranks of British society could opt for a more radical solution by joining the Fishing Fleet to India. It was an option that was taken by Jane Austen's aunt, Philadelphia Austen.

By the mid eighteenth century, the East India Company had become a powerful commercial trading organisation, effectively controlling all aspects of trade with India and much of South-East Asia and China. In 1774, Parliament passed a 'Regulatory Act' placing all aspects of government within India under the control of the East India Company, meaning anyone going to India needed permission from the Company. The number of East India officials, as well as standing armies in the Bengal, Bombay and Madras presidencies had increased rapidly, particularly attracting younger sons from among the aristocracy and gentry seeking career opportunities offering status and income. The problem facing the East India Company was that ultimately these young men would need wives – and they wanted English ones.

There was little opportunity within India itself. Contemporary estimates quoted by Katie Hickman in *She-Merchants, Buccaneers and Gentlewomen: British Women in India* indicates that for just the province of Bengal there were around 200 British women compared to around 250 East India Company officials, 4,000 British troops plus sundry tradesmen, merchants and seamen. The sheer distances between Britain and India and the fact that opportunities for a long leave back to Britain might only arise every five or six years meant finding a bride was difficult.

The East India Company came up with a solution and set out to encourage young single women to join its ships and travel to India in search of a husband. These ships became known as 'the Fishing Fleet'. Initially, the East India Company paid for their travel and basic maintenance for a few months to allow time for them to marry. By the late eighteenth century, this practice had changed and participants needed a sponsor to vouch for their good character and social status, as well as paying all their expenses. It was not a cheap option, with the Company charging young women £200 for passage on one of its vessels, which would also cover their initial maintenance.

In addition to this sum, the girl (or her sponsor) would have to pay for everything she would need during the voyage. The Company provided a cabin, although it was up to the girl to buy the furniture, soft furnishings, curtains, clothing and all other necessities, even a chamber pot, that she might need during the voyage.

It was a risky solution. Parents and sponsors sending girls to India might not know for a year or more whether they had arrived safely. Voyages to India could be extremely treacherous and could take up to eighteen months, depending on the route, which could involve sailing to the Canary Islands, then across to Brazil, back again to Africa, round the Cape of Good Hope, then across the Indian Ocean to India. There was a continual risk of being kidnapped by pirates and being held to ransom or being sold into slavery, succumbing to sickness or disease, being caught in sea battles, or suffering difficult weather conditions such as storms and hurricanes. Living conditions on board ship were difficult. Quite apart from all the passengers and crew on board there were also flocks of sheep and hens providing food en route. All these animals added to the noise and discomfort. Writing about her experiences on board a company ship, Charley Clive noted that sheep penned up on the poop deck fell through the ceiling and cascaded down into the room below. Girls had to accustom themselves to small, cramped insanitary rooms, boredom, coldness on deck and intense heat below deck. Remedies were few and far between if they fell ill, and many died before they reached their destination.

An alternative option involved a sea voyage to Egypt followed by travel overland across the desert to Suez, then another voyage to India. Eliza Fay was one such traveller who took this route in the eighteenth century and encountered reports of merchant caravans being attacked, plundered and people stripped of their clothes left to walk back across the desert in the scorching sun. She noted in her diary that when her party eventually arrived in Suez, the final voyage was equally difficult, with an extremely bad atmosphere involving argumentative passengers while the captain half-starved everyone on board.

Arrival in India came as a shock to most young women. Simply getting onto land could be hazardous. For many years, it was not always possible to dock the ship at a port with a harbour. Arriving in Madras, for example, required passengers to scramble into small lightweight bamboo canoes to travel across the waves, before being physically carried on the back of a fisherman to reach land. Canoes often broke up in the waves, resulting in passengers being injured or even killed.

Tysoe Hancock, a surgeon working in India, wrote of the dangers that faced the young women saying:

> You know very well that no Girl, tho' but fourteen years old, can arrive in India without attracting the Notice of every Coxcomb in the place, of whom there is plenty at Calcutta, with good Persons and no other Recommendation. Debauchery under the polite name of Gallentry is the reigning voice of the Settlement.

The brilliant colours, noise and excessive heat were added problems. The high humidity could destroy clothing and possessions such as books and shoes. In *She-Merchants, Buccaneers and Gentlewomen* Katie Hickman quotes Emma Roberts, who noted that furniture quickly became hot to the touch, with even the hardest wood liable to split as if hit by gunfire if not covered up by blankets. Insects were another hazard. There are contemporary references to furniture being eaten by termites, abundant cockroaches, slippers and shoes having to be shaken before being put on in order to remove any scorpions lurking inside.

Illness could strike quickly. In 1777 Jemima Kingsley, another girl who sought a husband via the Fishing Fleet wrote:

> the illness of which most people die is what is called here a Puker fever, which frequently carries a person off in a few hours, but some have a more lingering disease such as bile in the stomach which indeed is a disorder very few are exempt from in these cases; the intense heat relaxes the coats of the stomach so as to prevent digestion which occasions much illness and oft times death.

Even staying in a rented accommodation could be hazardous. One contemporary traveller recorded that on visiting a tavern in Madras he found seven people had died in his bed during the previous five weeks. The bed had not been aired, and the previous occupant had died in it just two days earlier. He decided against using the bed and chose to spend the night sleeping on top of a billiard table.

The risk of war and armed uprisings were always present. One such example was the Anjengo Affair (also known as the Anjengo Revolt). After founding a settlement and fort at Anjengo, the East India Company had sent annual gifts directly to the Rani of Attingal, but in 1721, the local chieftain demanded that the gifts for the Rani should be given to them to pass on. The East India Factor refused and sent 140 troops to accompany a delegation to Attingal for this purpose. The troops were attacked and massacred, with only twenty of the delegation said to have survived. Over the years there were many such encounters, including the Battle of Assaye (1803) and the Battle of Ferozeshah (1845).

By far the most notable example of such armed risings was the Indian Mutiny of 1857-59. Accusations of misrule and corruption by the East India Company became endemic and the British government became more involved, especially when British Army units began to be attached to the armies of the East India Company provinces. Discontent grew among local people, as well as Indian soldiers serving within the Bengal Army due to poor treatment, lack of promotion opportunities and greater cultural and racial insensitivity. The introduction of the Enfield rifle proved to be the catalyst for mutiny. Rumours spread that the cartridges used in the rifle were greased with pig and cow fat, materials that were offensive to Muslims and Hindus.

The mutiny began in 1857 when members of the Bengal Light Cavalry ransacked and killed a military fort, before taking control of Delhi. The revolt steadily spread, with some local rulers joining in as well as thousands of ordinary people unhappy with corruption and taxes. Thousands died throughout the revolt including British women and children. At Cawnpore in 1857, Major George Bingham reported that 'the place was literally running ankle deep in blood, ladies hair torn from their heads was lying about the floor; poor little children's shoes lying here and there ... after they had been killed, and even some alive, all were thrown down a deep well in the compound.'

In 1780, the *Bengal Gazette* wrote an account of what life was like for new arrivals to India and living in one of the cities. They were able to buy pastries and foodstuffs at the newly opened confectioners, meet friends in the Harmonic tavern, attend theatrical performances or buy a house. Women would spend their time shopping and making social visits to other English residents. After dinner at 2pm, they would take a siesta before heading to the racecourse. Evenings would be mainly spent at home drinking tea, playing cards and listening to music until supper at 10pm. Short formal visits would also often be made in the evening.

Women travelling as part of the Fishing Fleet quickly became part of local society. Writing in *She-Merchants, Buccaneers and Gentlewomen*, Katie Hickman reports that in 1798, Henrietta Clive, wife of the newly appointed Governor of Madras, commented on the sheer number of women who had arrived with the aim of finding a husband, saying, 'I really think I never saw so many females that had quite forgot what beauty might be. I have no idea of so many people assembled without one that would be thought tolerable in London.'

Newly arrived women were expected to marry as soon as possible. The arrival of a new Fishing Fleet vessel immediately attracted the attention of all single men in the area. They knew they had to act fast if they wanted a bride. Soon after arrival, girls were swept into a rapid social round of concerts, balls and picnics. Single men often moved fast if they found someone appealing – a proposal might be made within days of meeting, followed by a wedding equally quickly.

Over time, a more formal introduction structure emerged. Writing in her book *The Fishing Fleet: Husband Hunting in the Raj*, Anne de Courcy states:

> The arrival of a cargo of marriageable females was of intense interest to the numerous bachelors on the look out for a wife and ready to snap one up at the first opportunity. There was, however, an established ritual for this instant selection. The Captain of the ship, and well-known local ladies whose social credentials were beyond reproach would organise large parties at which the girls who hoped for a husband 'sat up' as it was called, for three or four nights in succession while the eligible bachelors, young and old, rushed there to look the cargo over and make an approach to the one who took their fancy. The church on Sundays was also a recognised venue for young men to try their luck.

> … What was left of the Fishing Fleet moved on to the mofussil (outlying districts) to scoop up husbands from the bunch of unmarried officials, soldiers, planters and businessmen who lived far from the great centres and, with less opportunity to find brides, were likely to be less choosy. With such a multitude of wife-seekers, a young woman had to be very plain or over-particular not to acquire a mate.

Some women in the Fishing Fleet would already have potential husbands awaiting them. This was the fate of Jane's aunt Philadelphia, the Reverend George Austen's older sister. After the death of their parents, Philadelphia and her younger sister Leonara went to live with their uncle, a London bookseller. On his death, the two girls were left destitute. Leonara opted to become a lady's companion while Philadelphia was facing employment as a London milliner. Her rich lawyer uncle, Old Francis Austen, suggested an alternative fate. He had a client in India – a surgeon named Tysoe Hancock – who needed a wife. Francis Austen offered to sponsor her to travel on an East India Company vessel out to India and become Hancock's bride. Philadelphia had little choice. Working as a London milliner was not well paid, nor would such a 'career' offer her much security and status.

In November 1751, Philadelphia became part of the Fishing Fleet, joining 112 other young ladies on the *Bombay Castle* travelling to India. Among the other girls on board was an orphan called Margaret Maskelyne, who also had a potential husband in view. She was travelling to India to join her brother, a soldier in the East India Company Army. Her brother had shown her portrait to a friend, Robert Clive, Governor of Bengal, who was immediately interested. As a result, Margaret's brother promptly wrote to her, saying he had found her a husband if she came quickly because 'she must make haste, as he is in such a marrying mood that I believe the first comer will carry him'.

On arrival in Madras, Margaret married Robert Clive within six months and enjoyed a happy married life, while Philadelphia Austen married Tysoe Hancock. Philadelphia's marriage was far less happy, at least according to her niece Jane, who later wrote saying, 'she had been … unhappily married … united to a man of double her own age, whose disposition was not amiable, and whose manners were unpleasing, though his character was respectable.'

Philadelphia enjoyed a luxurious lifestyle in Madras, but the marriage was childless. By 1759, the Hancocks had moved to Calcutta where Tysoe Hancock joined Warren Hastings, an administrator with the East India Company, in various business ventures. Warren Hastings had also married a Fishing Fleet girl who had come over to India at the same time as Philadelphia. Her name was Mary Elliot. She had initially married a soldier, but on his death had married Warren Hastings. Mary died in July 1759. Philadelphia found life in Calcutta more enjoyable, forging an active social life within the English community – and is reputed to have become the mistress of Warren Hastings, ultimately giving birth to his daughter, Eliza, in 1761. Such rumours immediately affected Philadelphia's reputation. Sir Robert Clive wrote to his wife Margaret demanding that 'In no circumstances whatever keep company with Mrs Hancock for it is beyond a doubt that she abandoned herself to Mr Hastings.'

Depending on where their husbands were based, it could be a lonely lifestyle for a new bride since some men were at stations or plantations outside the main cities and it was not unknown for there to be no other British women living in the area. Making friends with Indian women of similar status was rare since there was little social interaction between the two communities.

Despite this, life could be quite luxurious. British people living in India developed expensive tastes. Clothing was often lavish and expensive. Warren Hastings' second wife, Maria, was renowned for dressing extravagantly such as wearing satin riding habits trimmed with pearls and diamonds. On returning to England, such opulence was often ridiculed. In 1790, William Hickey prepared for a social occasion in London, choosing to wear 'one of my gay Indian coats, being of scarlet with a rich spangled and foil lace'. Instead of admiration, it resulted in comments that it was 'gaudy' and looked like 'the Lord Mayor's trumpeter'. Hickey quickly got rid of his Indian clothing. The London fashion for Indian muslins was never popular among Indian society because it was regarded as bad taste to wear anything manufactured locally.

There were always lots of servants to care for all aspects of life. Many households might have up to sixty servants or more, including gardeners, watercarriers, horse keepers, amatees (cleaners of silver and china), ayahs for the children, and messengers. When Maria Nugent joined her husband General Sir George Nugent, Commander in Chief of the East India Company Army in 1811 she discovered that her household consisted of over 100 servants, including four who stood behind her chair at every meal.

Any woman who could not find a husband, or who decided that life in India was not for them, became a 'Returned Empty', joining a ship bound for Britain. This was a fate rarely experienced by the first shiploads of young women, but as time went on, not all girls made the choice to stay.

Writing in *The Fishing Fleet*, Anne de Courcy gives the example of sisters Charlotte and Mary Britten, who joined the Fishing Fleet in 1821. Their brother George was already working for the East India Company, having gone out to India as a cadet in 1817. As the eldest of a family of thirteen children, he quickly realised the potential opportunities it posed for his sisters. On telling his parents of the opportunity, the decision was taken to send Charlotte (the fifth daughter) and Mary (the seventh daughter). As daughters of a London merchant, they were well born and well educated, making them ideal potential brides, and the girls set sail in January 1821. Among their fellow passengers were various authorised dependents plus a group of soldiers joining Indian regiments. Their voyage was relatively calm, apart from a birth on board to an 'authorised dependent', and a seaman having to be disciplined by receiving four dozen lashes with a cat o' nine tails.

On arrival in India, Charlotte (aged 21) decided to marry an East India Company official, 19-year-old Stuart Corbett, the son of Lady Augusta and the Reverend Corbett. Charlotte remained in India for the rest of her life, dying eighteen years later. Her husband returned on leave only once to England, in 1859. Charlotte's sister quickly chose to return to England on an East India Company ship as a 'Returned Empty'. She disliked India and was unhappy with the climate.

Opportunities for family life were limited. Wives tended to accompany husbands wherever they went and it was not unknown for military wives to give birth while moving from one base to another. It was also rare for children of Company staff to be raised in India. Children were usually returned to Britain and this could happen when they were babies, but always by the age of 7. They were placed in the care of people who happened to be travelling back, or even sent unaccompanied, care of the ship's captain. One such officer, Captain Hopkins of the *Seringapatum*, became known as the Bengal Ayah because so many children were sent back to England under his charge. Reasons for sending children back were based on a desire that they should not grow up with an Indian accent, and it was also felt that the climate at home would be healthier for them.

The experience of Warren Hastings' son, George, is typical. In 1761, he was sent back to Britain to be educated and fostered by an English family. George was given into the care of Cassandra Leigh's family, and when Cassandra married George Austen, George Hastings accompanied her to her new home, with Cassandra and George becoming his guardians. He stayed with them until his death from a 'putrid sore throat' in 1764. Warren Hastings only discovered that his son had died when he arrived in England the following year. The policy of sending children back to Britain continued for several decades, even after English schools were set up in India, as it was always felt better to have children educated back in England.

Sending surplus young women overseas became an increasingly popular option during the late eighteenth and nineteenth centuries, and it was a solution with which Jane Austen was all too familiar. She had grown up aware of the experiences of her aunt Philadelphia, the Fishing Fleet, and her subsequent life in India. The impact these stories had on Jane was considerable.

When she was just 16 years old, Jane wrote an unpublished story called *Catherine or The Bower*, which clearly echoes Philadelphia's experiences. The story focuses on the experiences of two girls, Catherine and Cecilia, within the marriage market. A rich relative pays for Cecilia to join the Fishing Fleet to India to find a husband. Meanwhile, Cecilia's younger sister chooses to stay in Britain and become a lady's companion. Although many of her friends believe that Cecilia has chosen the best option, Catherine is less convinced, highlighting the dangers that await Cecilia, commenting:

> Do you call it lucky, for a girl of genius and feeling to be sent in quest of a husband to Bengal, to be married there to a man whose disposition she has no opportunity of judging till her judgement is of no use to her, who may be a tyrant, or a fool or both for what she knows to the contrary. Do you call that fortunate?

Even at this young age, Jane was aware of the risks. Girls staying at home could at least seek advice from friends and relations as to the nature of the man they were marrying. If sent out to India, they were frequently faced with the prospect of having to decide rapidly, marrying almost complete strangers, unless they were fortunate enough to be marrying someone known to their family. The alternative was almost equally stark – if a girl could not find a husband in Britain, then there were few other options available beyond poverty, unless they had the contacts and references to gain a position as a lady's companion, governess or teacher in one of the many girls' schools.

The Indian option for surplus women continued throughout the nineteenth century. Society became much more structured, especially after the position of the East India Company was revoked, putting control directly under the British government. As Katie Hickman indicates in *She-Merchants, Buccaneers and Gentlewomen*, by the second half of the nineteenth century, it was a hierarchical society in which status depended on a husband's rank and position: 'a Warrant of Precedence dictated the social position of all English women from Vicereine to the wife of the lowliest Superintendent of Stamps and Stationery.'

As time went on, girls often travelled to India to visit relatives – and potentially gain a husband as well. Journeys were simpler and better organised. When joining their father in Madras, the daughters of Peter Cherry were given strict instructions as to what to bring, how to associate with other passengers and how to behave on board ship. By 1830 meals on board had become a formal process, requiring passengers to change before dinner. Lena Login joined her brother, an Army officer, in 1840. She travelled with her sister who was marrying an East India Company official. While travelling to Cawnpore to meet her brother, Lena met a bachelor serving as the Residency Surgeon at Lucknow. She married him and never joined her brother.

The opening of the Suez Canal in 1869 reduced the journey time from months to weeks, turning a trip to India into almost a holiday to explore the possibilities. Entire families often travelled there for the winter. A social calendar emerged, with balls, racing, dances, dinners and even visits to Indian spa towns. Some girls found husbands, but many now regarded it as just a pleasure trip.

Chapter 6

The Fate of Single Women

If a woman did not marry, then her future status and lifestyle was immediately at risk. Status was highly prized within Georgian society and affected all relationships and interactions with other people. The exact level of status possessed by a person depended very much on their wealth, name, background and behaviour. Women were ranked by their father's status, and later that of their husband.

In *Pride and Prejudice*, Lady Catherine de Burgh tells Elizabeth that

> My daughter and my nephew are formed for each other. They are descended on the maternal side from the same noble line; and, on the father's, from respectable, honourable and ancient, though untitled families. Their fortune on both sides is splendid. They are destined for each other by the voice of every member of their respective houses; and what is to divide them?

Elizabeth retorts that as Darcy is a gentlemen, and she is a gentleman's daughter, they are therefore equal in status, and while Lady Catherine accepts this, the status of Elizabeth's mother and her other relations is regarded as far less appealing as they are of professional status, thus lower in social rank.

Criticism of this situation had been made as early as 1792, when Mary Wollstonecraft published *A Vindication of the Rights of Women*. This was quite unique since it represented a woman writing about her own position in society. She argued that women deserved the same basic rights as men and should not be regarded just as ornaments to society and traded in marriage. Women, she argued, should also be given a decent education, commenting that, 'would men but generously snap our chains and be content with rational fellowship instead of slavish obedience, they would find us more observant daughters, more affectionate sisters, more faithful wives, more reasonable mothers – in a word, better citizens.'

Georgian society was relatively fluid. The ranks of the aristocracy remained small, with younger sons and daughters becoming members of the gentry within one or two generations. Intermarriage between the aristocracy and gentry was possible, with examples of this social fluidity being seen in Jane's own family. Her father was left penniless as a child but took advantage of the education his uncle provided to gain position and status within the Church. On her mother's side, the Duke of Chandos was her great great-uncle. The Leigh family were prosperous, but in choosing to marry into the lower ranks of the clergy, Cassandra Leigh was far less well off. Meanwhile, Jane's brother Edward gained position and wealth by being adopted as heir to the Knight fortune.

Women were aware that maintaining a good reputation was of paramount importance. The slightest slip could be fatal to a woman's reputation. Mary Bennett points out in *Pride and Prejudice* that a woman's reputation is 'no less brittle as it is beautiful'. In *Emma*, Harriet Smith stays on at Mrs Goddard's school as a parlour boarder, renting a room and using the parlour due to a lack of a better place to go. It gave her respectability, and she was able to present herself as eligible wife material.

A woman's status depended on how she behaved both in public and in private. It was all too easy to lose one's reputation, thus endangering her future prospects and status. Social engagements could be affected, with hostesses reluctant to send out invitations to parties, events and balls. In some circumstances it could result in being excluded from society altogether and have an adverse effect on relatives, especially unmarried girls; an immediate concern of Jane and Elizabeth following their sister Lydia's elopement in *Pride and Prejudice*.

Unmarried women, particularly younger ones, had very little freedom. A chaperone always had to be present when a woman was in the company of men. Women rarely went out unaccompanied. Jane Austen refers to walking to Deane one frosty day, even though it was only a mile away, but this was the first time she had ever done so on her own as she was usually accompanied by her sister or a maid. Opportunities for outside exercise were generally limited, unless they had a horse to ride. Women's footwear was generally unsuitable for walking any distance, especially given the muddy or dusty roads and paths that were common. The only alternative was to wear wooden clogs fastened over their soft shoes.

Whether married or single, women had little choice as to where they lived. When the Reverend George Austen decided to retire and move to Bath, he merely informed his wife and daughters of his decision. They had no say, but simply had to go where he decided they would live. No consideration was given to their needs, or the fact that they may not have been able to take cherished possessions, including books and music sheets, with them. Most of the family possessions were sold at this point. Auction details printed in the *Reading Mercury* include references to Jane's piano, a collection of music, books, pictures and furniture. Judging by Jane's letters to Cassandra, the idea of moving to Bath was not immediately pleasing. It was not until January 1801 that she wrote to Cassandra:

> I get more and more reconciled to the idea of our removal. We have lived long enough in this neighbourhood, the Basingstoke Balls are certainly on the decline, there is something interesting in the bustle of going away, and the prospect of spending future summers by the Sea or in Wales is very delightful.

As Lucy Worsley points out in *Jane Austen at Home*, 'it was something all unmarried young ladies could expect. Mary (James's wife) had herself been ripped from her childhood home of Deane Parsonage, and in due course, she too would have to leave the Rectory to give way for the next generation.'

Single women without any private income and declining marriage prospects understandably feared the future. There was a definite social stigma linked to being a spinster. William Hayley's *Essay on Old Maids* indicated clearly what could await the unmarried daughters of gentlemen, saying, 'It is probable that after having passed the sprightly years of youth in the comfortable mansion of an opulent father, she is reduced to the shelter of some contracted lodging in a country town, attended by a single servant.'

He added that such spinsters also had 'to be embittered by their disappointment in the great object of female hope' i.e. to marry and have children.

An Old Maid was often seen as a figure of fun, even when they were gainfully employed. Governess Nelly Weeton noted that 'an old maid is a stock for everyone to laugh at. Boys play tricks upon them, and are applauded. Girls sneer at them, and are unreproved. Upon my word, I think I will write an essay upon the pitiable state of old maids.' In *Emma*, when Harriet Smith points out that Emma Woodhouse is likely to end up like Miss Bates if she insists on not marrying, Emma responds: 'Never mind, Harriet, I shall not be a poor old maid; and it is poverty only which makes celibacy contemptible to a generous public! A single woman with a very narrow income must be a ridiculous, disagreeable, old maid! The proper sport of boys and girls.'

Jane Austen was all too aware of the problems, writing in a letter to Fanny Knight in 1817 that 'Single women have a dreadful propensity for being poor – which is one very strong argument in favour of Matrimony.' She knew that on their father's death, she and her sister would face serious economic problems. For spinsters, the risk of poverty was never far away. When living at Chawton, Jane met Mary Benn, the very poor sister of the Reverend John Benn, rector of the nearby parish of Farringdon. Mary's clothing had become threadbare and Jane's friend, Martha Lloyd, had expressed a wish to give Mary a present. In 1812, Jane wrote to Martha saying that a shawl would be useful 'to wear over her shoulders within doors in very cold weather … Her long fur tippet is almost worn out.' Ultimately, Mary would be evicted from her cottage.

References to 'years of danger', when single women in their twenties had not found a husband despite being out in society, are frequently made in the literature of the time, including Jane Austen's novels. In *Persuasion*, Elizabeth Elliot 'had the consciousness of being nine-and-twenty to give her some regrets and some apprehensions: she was fully satisfied of being still quite as handsome as ever, but she felt her approach to the years of danger.'

Spinsters among the gentry and aristocracy possessed a subordinate position within any household. They were dependent on others and had no personal rights. They risked being reduced to the status of a surplus aunt, called on to help out with the care of nephews and nieces, especially when they were ill or their mother was expecting another child. Both Jane and Cassandra frequently visited their brother Edward Knight, spending weeks at his home and while there helping with the children. They were constantly moving, as required, from one household to another, from brother to brother, married sister to married sister. Alternatively, they might be expected to act as a hostess in an unmarried brother's household. This is the position taken by Miss Caroline Bingley in *Pride and Prejudice* – but as soon as her brother marries, her role as hostess would no longer exist.

Around two thirds of women in the eighteenth century are estimated to have been single, and although many were widows, a large proportion of these single women were unmarried. This remained the norm during the nineteenth century, with the number of available men actually decreasing as the decades passed. In the time of the 1841 Census, Bath had 10,767 spinsters to 4,057 bachelors. By 1853, 43 percent of women in England were recorded as being single. Quite apart from the issue of finding a husband, in reality there were simply not enough men available. Younger sons of aristocracy, gentry and professional classes were equally short of cash and unable to afford a wife and family.

Becoming a governess was one of the few options open to young, single women who had been born and brought up as the daughters of gentlemen such as the clergy. They had a desirable status as gentlewomen – but no money. If they did not marry, then they were left with few choices as to their future life.

Gently born women, even aristocratic women, had worked as governesses for several centuries. In Tudor England, Lady Kat Ashley acted as the governess of Princess Elizabeth (later Elizabeth I). As such she was responsible for the welfare and initial education of the young princess, as well as acting as her chaperone and companion as she grew older. By the eighteenth century, the work of a governess had begun to change so as to focus on the education of girls at home, teaching them basic skills and the attributes that they would need for their future lives as wives and mothers. Gently born women – especially the daughters of clergymen – who had the necessary status as well as experiencing a similar education were regarded as ideal. *The Complete Servant* by Samuel Adams (1825) noted that a governess 'should be able to conduct herself in such a manner, as never to render an apology necessary for her presence at family parties.'

The availability of governess positions depended on who you knew, your family and social connections. If you were lucky, it was a life that could be reasonably rewarding financially. Much depended on the kindness of their employers. In *Emma*, Miss Taylor (Emma's governess) was treated as a member of the family and after marrying later became Mrs Weston. Most governesses were less lucky.

An advertisement for a governess in the *Bath Chronicle* in 1798 read:

> She is expected to rise early, and will not have a maid to attend her. She is to sleep in the room with a Young Lady, and to eat with her when requested. The salary Sixty Guineas a year – She will not visit with the Lady (of the house) as she is wanted to attend entirely to the education of two Young Ladies.

Actual examples of single women who managed to create a reasonable lifestyle as a governess are rare. Agnes Porter (1750-1814) is one such lady. Her father was a clergyman who struggled to maintain his wife and three daughters. Letters and diaries written by Agnes and published under the tile *A Governess in the Age of Jane Austen: the Journals and Letters of Agnes Porter* indicated that she had hoped to marry, but with no dowry she had little option but to seek an alternative solution. She was aware of the risks awaiting her writing that: 'I could not forbear partially and deeply reflecting on the ills that single women are exposed to, even at the hour of death, from being the property of no one.'

Being reasonably well educated, speaking fluent French and playing the piano and harpsichord, Agnes found work as a governess through her social connections. During her life she became a governess within several prominent families, including spending twenty years educating the children and grandchildren of the second Earl of Ilchester. In her notebooks she recorded her lifestyle and how she coped as a governess. The Earl of Ilchester was unusual in that he had some fondness for his children and liked taking them out. Agnes was left with free time to entertain friends in her private rooms. She was allowed to dine with the family and spend her evenings with them. Despite this, life could be lonely, as she noted in her journal, 'When Lord Ilchester is from home, I spend the evenings with his daughters; when he is at home I pass them alone.'

While working within the Ilchester household, she earned around £105 a year from which she managed to save some money. Agnes eventually moved on to work for the Talbot family at Penrice Castle between 1799-1806, where she was paid £100 a year. Such sums were regarded as being very generous – especially since the two families also provided annuities once she was too old to work.

However, these annuities also highlighted the problem that could arise regarding payment. After leaving the Ilchester household, Agnes was given an annuity of £30 a year, but this ceased on the death of the earl due to the sheer size of his personal debts. There was no money available to pay any legacies such as the annuity due to Agnes, and she was unlikely to be able to get anything until the new Earl of Ilchester came of age in 1808. Agnes was greatly concerned about the situation and contacted her former employer's brother. She notes, 'I asked the Colonel what I was to do in the interval, and added that should I from ill health be obliged to give up my profession and be reduced to want, I thought it would be reflection on his noble family.' His response was clearly unsatisfactory since she later wrote, 'He seemed to think what I said was une façon de parler – but he knows not me.'

Forced to give up work in 1806, Agnes received £30 a year as a pension from the Talbot family, and a home with her sister and brother-in-law at Fairford. The annuity from Lord Ilchester was finally resumed in 1808. By the end of her life in 1814, Agnes had a yearly income of around £150, of which around £100 came from monies totalling £2,000 invested in 5 percent Navy Stock.

The experience of Agnes was unusual. If you were unlucky in your choice of situation, and did not have the right connections, then your position in life could be difficult. This was unfortunately true for most governesses. The work of a governess was increasingly perceived as being poorly paid and of low status, being neither family nor servant but something in between. *The Complete Servant* noted that a governess had to be able to 'conduct herself in such a manner, as never to render an apology necessary for her presence at family parties' but she was always aware that she was not part of the family and could lose her position at short notice.

For single women living within a family, and girls being educated, the presence of a governess in the household was a constant reminder that any gently born woman could easily face the same fate. They did not fit in with servants, even upper servants like housekeepers, butlers and nannies simply because as governesses, they came from a higher social status. Numerous references to this difficult status can be found in literature and archives throughout the late eighteenth and nineteenth centuries.

For example, Mary Wollstonecraft hated working as a governess to the daughters of Lord Viscount Kingsborough, writing that she was 'above the servants, yet considered by them as a spy … shut out from equality and confidence'. She recognised the difficulty of her situation since as a governess, noting 'I should be shut out from society and be debarred the imperfect pleasures of friendship – as I should on every side be surrounded by unequals.'

Georgian governess Nelly Weeton worked with families in Ambleside and Huddersfield. She noted in her diary, 'I sit alone in the evening, in the schoolroom there is nobody in the house with whom I can be on equal terms, and I know nobody out it.' She concluded that 'a governess is more a prisoner than any servant in the house.'

Nelly also noted in her diary the limitations on accommodation provided for a governess, reporting that her bedroom was '7 feet by 9, with a bed, a chest of drawers, two chairs and a wash-stand in it (don't peep under the bed now!) with just spare room for myself and the fire, and a tea-tray put over the wash-stand to serve for a table'. Despite this, she did enjoy 'many a snug sit' and 'a fire in my room on a cold winter's evening, was one of the greatest comforts I had.'

By the mid nineteenth century, having a private governess for one's children had become a status symbol in genteel households. Their position did not improve. In 1848, William Makepeace Thackeray's novel *Vanity Fair* contains a comment by the cook, who states 'I don't like them governesses. They give themselves the hairs and hupstarts of ladies, and their wages is no better than you nor me.'

Jane Austen was aware of the problems of being a governess. Although she had personally escaped that fate, the comments made by Jane Fairfax in *Emma* indicate that she understood the difficulties of their lives: 'With the fortitude of a devoted novitiate, she had resolved at one-and-twenty to complete the sacrifice and retire from all the pleasures of life, of rational intercourse, equal society, peace and hope to penance and mortification forever.' Jane Fairfax later goes on to compare the governess trade to being comparable to the slave trade. She could not hope to improve her situation and there would be few opportunities, if any, to meet suitable men.

A further problem for governesses was the fact that as unprotected single women, they were regarded as fair game by male guests and other menfolk within the household. Seduction and rape were all too common. As a result, they would lose their situation, and have to deal with the results of the liaison in the form of an unwanted pregnancy.

For the majority of governesses, pay was low. While working in Westmorland in 1808, Ellen Weeton was paid just 30 guineas (just over £31) per annum. In 1841, Charlotte Bronte worked as a governess for just £20 a year. The general lack of provision for aged, infirm former governesses steadily became a serious problem, leading to the development of the Governesses Benevolent Institution in 1843.

If not working as a governess, the main occupation for single gently born ladies, or widows in need of an income was that of a companion. In order to be accepted for such a position, a woman had to be gently born and of a similar background to that of their employer. Such companions might be employed to work in the households of widows seeking company, a married woman who sought female company, wealthy unmarried women living on their own, or to act as a chaperone to a younger woman since it was socially unacceptable to receive male visitors without an older woman or male relative being present. The task of a companion was very much a social one, helping to entertain guests and accompany the lady of the house to social events, providing company and conversation when required. In return, a companion would receive a small allowance, accommodation and would eat with the family.

Positions as a companion might be acquired as a result of recommendations from gentry families or clergy, or by answering advertisements placed in quality newspapers. All such advertisements emphasised than prospective companions had to be highly skilled, of appropriate birth and possess a good reputation.

Judging by Jane Austen's letters, she was well aware of the existence of companions and she encountered many when out in society. One such woman was Mrs Stent, the companion of Mrs Lloyd. In a letter to Cassandra in 1805, Jane describes her as being 'of rather inferior position in life, and reduced from family misfortune, to very narrow means.' She pities her and recognises that such a fate awaits any single woman saying, 'Poor Mrs Stent! It has been her lot to be always in the way, but we must be merciful, for perhaps in time we may come to be Mrs Stents ourselves, unequal to anything and unwelcome to everybody.'

In *Pride and Prejudice*, Mrs Jenkinson acts as the companion to Anne De Bough, Lady Catherine's daughter and Mr Darcy's cousin. Her life is clearly an unpleasant one. She has to do everything that Lady Catherine and Anne require and has no privacy at all. Lady Catherine tells Elizabeth that she can use the piano in Mrs Jenkinson's room whenever she likes. Mrs Jenkinson has no say in the matter and cannot set times or circumstances.

For many other single women possessing less status, there was little choice but to become a prostitute in order to survive. It was an option that brought immediate risks in terms of serious venereal diseases as well as unwanted pregnancies. Laws against prostitution were loosely enforced. There were laws against keeping brothels but prostitution itself was not made an imprisoning offence until the 1820s. There are no reliable statistics as to the number of prostitutes in existence during the Regency period, although various historians have suggested estimates ranging from 20,000 to 50,000. Dan Cruickshank's *The Secret History of Georgian London* reckons that up to one in five women in London earned an income from prostitution, ranging from high class women catering for the aristocracy to the common prostitutes found in working class streets. Often it was a way of supplementing income from occupations such as seamstresses and milliners. Sir John Fielding, magistrate of the Bow Street Police Court, described Covent Garden as 'the great square of Venus' in which 'one would imagine that all the prostitutes in the kingdom had picked upon the rendezvous.'

Flora Tristan, an aristocrat and feminist linked to a prominent Peruvian family visiting England in the early nineteenth century, wrote in her journal about watching the activities of prostitutes starting their day in the West End. She followed their activities as they sought customers while walking the streets of Mayfair and Westminster, before steadily descending further and further through society ending in the 'finishes' or gin palaces which were 'vast, sumptuous taverns where one goes to finish out the night.' Tristan concludes her account with the words, 'Towards midnight the habitués begin to arrive. Several of these taverns are the meeting places for high society where the elite of the aristocracy assembles … The orgy is steadily rising to a crescendo, between four and five o'clock in the morning it reaches its peak.'

Throughout her life, Jane Austen never had much money to spare. Her personal allowance was just £20 a year. Her diaries reflect the careful attention she paid to spending what little funds she had. While shopping in Bath during a visit in 1799, she wrote to Cassandra saying:

> Though you have given me unlimited powers concerning your Sprig I cannot determine what to do about it … we have been to the cheap shop, and very cheap we found it, but there are only flowers there, no fruit and as I could get 4 or 5 very pretty sprigs of the former for the same money which would procure only one Orleans plumb, in short could get more for three or four shillings than I could have means of bringing home … Besides I cannot help thinking that it is more natural to have flowers grow out of the head than fruit.

In 1807, Jane noted in her diary that she started the year with £50 15s 6d. At the end of year, she had just £6 4s 6d. Typical expenses during the year had included a journey to Chawton costing £1 2s 10d; £13 19s 3d on clothing; washing £9 5s 11½d; presents £6 4s 4d, charity payments of £3 10s 3½d, and the hire of pianoforte costing £2 13s 6d. Although very difficult to compare with modern financial equivalents, £50 would amount to approximately £5,760, meaning after all expenses are deducted, Jane would have been left with just under £700.

Creating a career as a female author was unusual. The number of female writers was quite small, with many adopting a male pseudonym or opting for anonymity. In 1801, Mary Hays, a widow, author and friend of Mary Wollstonecraft, noted that 'the penalties and discouragements attending the profession of an author fall upon women with a double weight.' She believed that they were 'tried in the court of public opinion, not merely as writers, but as women, their characters, their conduct' constantly under scrutiny with people seeking to identify 'their errors and exposing their foibles'. At one point there were even suggestions being made that the most famous female writer of the time, Ann Radcliffe, author of *The Mysteries of Udolpho*, had gone insane.

Initially Jane had written for fame, without any view to earning any money from her work, but the situation changed as she became aware of the possibilities. Although she had written stories all her life, her family did not regard her as a writer. Only men were expected to be writers and have works published. Jane's brother James was regarded as the writer in the family due to the theological books he had written. His sister's domestic skills were regarded as being far more important than her writing. According to her other brother, Henry Austen, Jane was:

> careful that her occupation should not be suspected by servants, or visitors, or any persons beyond her own family – she wrote upon small sheets of paper which could easily be put away, or covered with a sheet of blotting paper. There was, between the front door and the offices, a swing door that creaked when it was opened, but she objected to having this little inconvenience remedied, because it gave her notice when anyone was coming.

Jane's initial attempts at publication did not meet with great success. Without her knowledge, her father contacted Thomas Cadell, a London publisher, regarding a publishing deal for her novel *First Impressions* (later renamed *Pride and Prejudice*). Cadell refused, returning his letter marked 'Declined by Return of Post'. No further attempts were made to publish her work until Jane asked her brother Henry to act as her literary agent. In 1803 he offered *Susan* to Benjamin Crosby, a London publisher. Crosby paid £10 for the copyright and advertised the book as being 'in the press'. It never went any further. In 1809 Jane sought to regain ownership of *Susan*, but Crosby argued that he had never agreed to publish it at any specific point in time and if she wanted the novel, she would have to buy it back at the cost of £10; a sum Jane could not afford.

Jane turned her attention to editing her novel *Elinor and Marianne* so as to bring it up to date, changing references such as the cost of postage to London, and in the meantime renaming it *Sense and Sensibility*. Thomas Egerton, a publisher known to Henry Austen through his military connections, accepted the book for publication. Jane's identity was kept secret and she was not named as the author. The book was described as being written 'by a lady'. Such anonymity was the usual custom of the period. If a female writer rejected anonymity, they usually claimed it was due to having reasons for needing to make money such as an invalid husband or destitute children.

Sense and Sensibility was published 'on commission', a normal method of publication at this time. This meant that Jane was liable for any losses that were incurred but did receive a share of the profits. In preparation for this possibility, Jane reserved £180 from her very small annual income since this would be enough to cover publication. It was money that she could not really afford, and if required it would probably have needed Henry's help in order to pay such a debt. Taking into account publication costs, the publishers would expect to make a profit of £35 from the book, while the most Jane could expect from those 750 copies that were printed was £140. When the book was published in October 1811, *Sense and Sensibility* quickly sold out.

Given the success of her first book, the publishers purchased the copyright of her second novel, *Pride and Prejudice*. For Jane, this turned out to be a bad choice as the publishers benefited, gaining a higher income than Jane did. *Pride and Prejudice* became the most talked about book of the season in 1813, resulting in everyone wanting to read it. Writing to her mother, Anne Milbanke (who later married Lord Byron), commented 'I really think it is the most probable fiction I have ever read'.

Sales of Jane's books hit problems in 1816. Henry was declared bankrupt and Jane lost £12 from the second edition of *Sense and Sensibility*, plus £13 profits from *Mansfield Park*. Two thousand copies of *Emma* were published at the same time as the second edition of *Mansfield Park*, and both books were competing for the same readers. The losses incurred on *Mansfield Park*'s second edition virtually cancelled out all the profits on *Emma*. That same year, she also repurchased the copyright of *Susan* from the publishers Benjamin Crosby, who had never done anything with it. This allowed her to begin revising it for future publication elsewhere.

A second edition of *Sense and Sensibility* brought in a further £20 from the publishers. Jane only received £8 13s in royalties for *Emma*, despite it gaining good reviews from well-known society figures such as Sir Walter Scott, who wrote in the *Quarterly Review* of 1815 that it was 'a correct and striking representation of that which is daily taking place'. *Emma* was never liked as much as Jane's other novels. After the initial flurry of sales, the final 539 copies were eventually remaindered four years later.

By comparison with other authors of the period, Jane's income from writing was very low. Lucy Worsley points out in her book that 'Jane could not have afforded to live entirely by her pen in anything like the style to which she was accustomed. She was never to even approach being wealthy from her work, earning a lifetime total of only around £668.'

Her income was low by any standards. An agricultural labourer in 1814 earned £40 a year, while a solicitor earned £1,500. Other novelists of the period were known to have earned significant sums from their writing – Frances Burney gained £4,000 while Maria Edgeworth earned £11,000, becoming one of the most successful female novelists of the time.

Even though Jane's books were quickly translated and published overseas, she gained nothing in return. There was no international copyright available and the books were changed to suit their readership. *Pride and Prejudice* was published in January 1813 in London and by March 1813 work was underway by a Swiss company translating copies acquired in London, who published it in four instalments. The storyline was adjusted to suit Swiss readers, making Elizabeth far less vivacious and much more demure and obedient to her mother.

So why did Jane experience so little financial success? Establishing yourself as an author was not easy. Female authors tended to be treated fairly unsympathetically, unless they had the support of a male relative. Some female writers preferred to stay anonymous. This was the case of Elizabeth and Jane Purbeck, two sisters who were both unmarried. They published six novels anonymously.

In 1801, dissenter and writer Mary Hays noted, 'the penalties and discouragements attending the profession of an author fall upon women with a double weight.' Impressed by Wollstonecraft's *Vindication of the Rights of Women*, Hays took the extremely unusual step for a Georgian lady of leaving her mother's home to live independently in London because she wanted to take charge of her own life. She commented that women authors were subject to public opinion 'not merely as writers, but as women, their characters, their conduct' coming under scrutiny with 'malignant ingenuity' designed to 'expose their foibles'.

A key part of Jane's financial problems lay in her publishing agreements. From the beginning, poor choices were made and she never really recovered from this. Her situation was compounded by the problems encountered by her brother's unwise financial decisions, which eventually rendered him bankrupt. Her family's continual financial problems meant that Jane had to postpone printing either *Persuasion* or *Susan* and her ill health further added to her difficulties. *Persuasion* was eventually publisher after her death and sold well. In 1832, Richard Bentley acquired the copyright to all her novels and quickly published collected and illustrated editions. Since then, they have never been out of print.

Chapter 7

The Fate of Surplus Sons

It was not just daughters who experienced issues regarding their future in the late eighteenth and early nineteenth century. Most sons also faced uncertain futures. In *Pride and Prejudice*, Colonel Fitzwilliam tells Elizabeth that 'A younger son, you know, must be inured to self-denial and dependence ... in matters of greater weight, I may suffer from the want of money. Younger sons cannot marry where they like.' Finding a bride with money often solved many problems, which is why younger sons could be very active on the London social circuit.

The practice of primogeniture meant that property normally passed to the eldest son. Unless the family was sufficiently wealthy to make some kind of provision for younger sons, those younger sons could only inherit if the oldest son died leaving no direct descendants. Since parents often had multiple children, this meant that most sons faced the prospect of having to find some form of employment. Traditionally, in aristocratic families, this meant the oldest son would inherit the land, the next son would become a clergyman, while the next was destined for the Army, followed by the law.

University education was essential for careers in the Church and legal professions. This could be very expensive, involving tuition and accommodation for ten years or more. The Austen family were fortunate in this respect. Cassandra Austen (née Leigh) was descended from the family of the founder of St John's College, Oxford, Sir Thomas White, which meant her sons could claim Founder's Kin fellowships. Two of the boys took up this opportunity. James Austen joined the college as a fellow in 1779, took his BA in 1783, MA in 1788 and was ordained as a priest in 1789. He resigned his fellowship in 1792 when he married and acquired a living. Henry Austen, meanwhile, joined St John's in 1788, taking a BA in 1792 and an MA in 1796. He resigned his fellowship in 1796 after choosing to join the Militia and married the following year.

Careers in the church, military and law did come at a price, however. It was expensive to send boys to university, since this was an essential requirement for careers in both the church and the law, while commissions in the Army, even at the lowest level, had to be purchased. Moving from one rank to another came at a price – just moving from the lowest officer grade of cornet to a lieutenant cost £50. Obtaining a commission or rank within a prestigious regiment would cost more; a lieutenant colonel could cost as much as £4,000. In *Pride and Prejudice*, Mr Darcy has to buy George Wickham an Army commission costing around £450, as well as paying his debts and providing a dowry for Lydia in order to persuade him to marry her.

Frank Austen opted for a career in the Royal Navy and was followed in due course by his brother Charles. Their choice of career resulted in a very different lifestyle and environment to that which they were accustomed as children living in a rural rectory, since life in the Royal Navy was extremely hard. Despite this, it did offer considerable potential career opportunities, coming at a time when Britain and France were at war. This offered scope for advancement as well as making money. Everything depended on luck and family connections, as well as surviving participation in the inevitable battles.

Life in the Royal Navy was not easy. Many of the crew were unwilling participants, having been press ganged into service. This practice related to the fact that the Crown claimed the right to seize men of seafaring experience for service in the Royal Navy. During naval wars, this was frequently given extra force by Acts of Parliament, known as the Impressment Acts, such as the one passed in 1779.

The activities of the press gang and the acts of impressment often led to riots.

Most pressed men were usually fishermen and sailors from merchant fleets within coastal towns and dockland areas, although it was not unknown for apprentices and labourers from elsewhere to be pressed. Convicted criminals could also be pressed. The only way of avoiding the activities of a press gang was to flee and keep out of sight. The press gang received a bounty for every pressed man, and judging by figures from the Impressment Service it has been estimated that over half of the 120,000 sailors serving in the Royal Navy during the Battle of Trafalgar in 1805 were pressed men.

Once pressed, these reluctant members of the Royal Navy had no choice but to serve for as long as required. As crew members, they were not always amenable to life within the Navy and jumping ship when in port was all too frequent. Punishments could be very severe and result in considerable suffering. Flogging using a cat o' nine tails (a whip with nine waxed knotted tails) was the most common and was witnessed by the whole crew. Twelve lashes were the usual punishment, but some captains would charge a sailor with multiple offences each incurring an additional twelve lashes. A ship's doctor of the period noted that just twelve lashes could leave a man's back 'swollen like a pillow, looking black-and-blue'. Such punishments would have been witnessed and sometimes supervised by officers like Frank and Charles Austen from the moment they joined their ships as midshipmen. In 1813, Frank was admonished for the level of punishments he had given the crew on board HMS *Elephant*.

Life on board ship was definitely not for the faint hearted. Sailors were often malnourished despite ships being well supplied with dried food, cheese, beef, pork, hard tack biscuits and gruel. Fresh fruit and vegetables were generally in short supply, however, especially on long voyages. There was a constant risk of illness and death. Living in cramped and damp conditions, fevers were common. Infectious diseases like smallpox, measles, tuberculosis and typhus spread quickly within the close conditions, while crews stationed in the West Indies often suffered from malaria. Jane's sister Cassandra's fiancée, Tom Fowle, died from yellow fever while accompanying Lord Craven to the West Indies and was buried at sea. Syphilis and gonorrhoea were also common.

Scurvy was a perennial problem resulting in sailors suffering from putrid gums, rotting wounds, weak muscles, swellings and lassitude. It was generally accepted that on a long voyage, around 50 percent of sailors would die of scurvy. Research by Dr James Lind serving on board HMS *Salisbury* eventually identified the cause as being due to lack of fresh fruit and vegetables. By 1795, another physician, Gilbert Blane, had convinced the Royal Navy to issue lemon and lime juice to sailors, a decision which proved crucial in enabling ships to spend months at sea without suffering from scurvy.

During battle, amputations were common, being the only solution for limbs smashed by cannon balls. The speed by which an amputation was carried out could make the difference between life and death, resulting in surgeons working extremely quickly. The death rate during a battle was high; naval records indicate that at the Battle of Trafalgar, 1,500 seamen were killed during five hours of constant fighting.

Mutinies did occur. In April 1797, sailors serving on board sixteen ships of the Channel Fleet commanded by Admiral Lord Bridport refused to set sail from Spithead. They complained about living conditions, demanded a pay rise, better food, more shore leave and compensation for sickness and injury. They also sought the removal of unpopular officers. Within days, fifteen ships at Plymouth joined in the mutiny, sending delegates to the negotiations. The mutiny finally ended when Admiral Lord Howe intervened, offering a royal pardon for all crews involved, the reassignment of unpopular officers, and a pay rise.

The following month, sailors on the Nore, an anchorage on the Thames Estuary, also mutinied. This proved to be a much more serious mass mutiny, with Royal Navy flags being replaced with red flags. The mutineers demanded more shore leave, a fairer distribution of prize money and changes to the Articles of War. In order to achieve their demands, they sought to impose a blockage on the Thames, preventing vessels from reaching London, but the Admiralty refused to give in and the government, under William Pitt the Younger, introduced a bill to outlaw the mutineers. After being denied food and water, the Nore mutiny fell apart and several ships returned to duty and quietly sailed to Sheerness. Richard Parker, the leader of the mutineers, hoisted a signal to sail to France, but the remaining ships refused to follow him. There was no forgiveness this time. Richard Parker was court-martialled and executed by being hung from the yardarm of HMS *Sandwich*. Naval records indicate that twenty-one mutineers were also hanged, twenty-nine were imprisoned and nine were flogged. Several others were transported to Australia.

For young men like Frank and Charles Austen who chose a naval career, training began at Portsmouth Naval College. According to Claire Tomalin, author of *Jane Austen: A Life*, 'the regime there was tough, not to say brutal; discipline was maintained with a horsewhip, and there were complaints about bullying, idleness and debauchery.'

Frank was only 12 years old when he joined the College. His younger brother Charles joined it five years later. As trainees, they had to study all aspects of naval life including handling sails, mapping, navigation, gunnery, mathematics, maritime law and meteorology. When their training was complete, they signed up as midshipmen. Serving as midshipmen on board a naval vessel meant they would be junior officers living in the gunroom and responsible for a variety of tasks such as keeping watch, running the ship's boats and helping with navigation. It was not unknown for midshipmen to stay in this role for years, even after gaining the skills and experience needed for ranks such as lieutenant and captain. In order to rise to higher ranks in the Royal Navy, the right connections were needed. Men in their thirties could still be in the position of midshipmen due to their lack of patronage.

In *Mansfield Park*, William Price describes himself as being a 'poor scrubby midshipman' and that 'one is nothing indeed'. William had only gained his initial position due to the efforts of his uncle, Sir Thomas Bertram, who had 'done the most for his support and advancement'. Seeking to advance his personal relationship with Fanny Price, Henry Crawford asks his uncle, Admiral Crawford, to promote William to the rank of lieutenant. In *Persuasion*, meanwhile, Admiral Croft reacts to Captain Wentworth's complaints about being given command of the sloop *Asp* by telling him that he was a 'lucky fellow to get anything so soon, with no more interest than his'.

Such references reflect the reality of life for a young officer or would-be officer in the Royal Navy, where there were often more than 2,000 young men seeking advancement. Jane Austen was all too aware of the situation. Both Frank and Charles were helped by their family connections to develop their naval careers. In 1794, the Reverend Austen contacted his friend, Warren Hastings, the former Governor General of India. Hastings was the godfather (and probable father) of Jane's cousin Eliza (who later married Henry Austen). Mr Austen asked Hastings to use his contacts with First Naval Lord Affleck to help Frank Austen gain a position in the Royal Navy.

As the years passed, other family connections came into play. One of the strongest naval connections that the Austen family possessed was thanks to the links it had with the Matthew family. The first wife of the Reverend James Austen (Jane's eldest brother) was Anne Matthew, daughter of General Edward Matthew, who had served as Governor of Grenada. Two of Anne's nieces married brothers from the Gambier family: James (who became a Lord Commissioner of the Admiralty and First Naval Lord) and Samuel (Secretary of the Navy Board). Frank Austen served under James Gambier on several ships and this connection led to Frank's initial promotions.

In December 1798, Jane wrote to Cassandra saying that their father was about to write to James Gambier concerning their brother Charles, commenting 'he will be delighted to have another Austen to help'. A few days later, Jane wrote another letter to her sister saying that James Gambier had indicated Charles would be moved to a larger ship 'when a proper opportunity offers and it is judged that he has taken his Turn in a small ship'. Gambier also indicated in his letter to the Reverend Austen that as a result of information he had received from Lord Spencer of the Admiralty, 'I can give you the assurance that his promotion is likely to take place very soon'. On 28 December 1798, Jane wrote again to Cassandra saying that 'Frank is made. – He was yesterday raised to the Rank of Commander, and appointed to the Petterel sloop, now at Gibraltar' and that 'Lieut. Charles Austen is removed to the Tamar frigate'.

The Austen links to the Gambier family ultimately led to a connection with Lord Moira, a senior military commander and companion to the Prince Regent. Captain Charles James was Lord Moira's financial agent, as well as being Henry Austen's banking partner. Henry Austen's bank (Austen, Maunde & Tilson) lent money to Lord Moira in return for support in advancing the careers of both Frank and Charles Austen. In 1803-04 Lord Moira received loans amounting to £2,000 from Henry Austen. In turn, Moira's support led to Charles to gaining his first command, the sloop *Indian* based in Bermuda. Similar loans in return for letters were granted in 1805 in the hope of gaining a frigate for Frank Austen, but were not successful.

Charles Austen's naval career also benefited from another family connection. Jane's cousin, Jane Cooper, married Captain Thomas Williams (later Admiral Williams). He became the patron of Charles Austen and it was while serving on Admiral Williams' ship that Charles was promoted to lieutenant following the Battle of Camperdown, off the coast of Holland in 1797.

Losing a patron, or simply being in the wrong place at the wrong time, could have serious consequences on career prospects. This is exactly what happened to Frank Austen in 1805. In late October, he was sent on a supply run to Gibraltar. Unfortunately, this meant he was not with the main Royal Navy fleet when it engaged the French and Spanish fleets at Cape Trafalgar on 21 October. When he returned to the fleet with the required supplies, he discovered his patron Lord Nelson had died in battle, and that those captains who had taken part in the Battle of Trafalgar were now receiving significant rewards and lucrative posts. Writing to his fiancée Mary, he noted the impact it had made on his life:

> I shall ever consider the day on which I sailed away from the Squadron as the most inauspicious one of my life … Alas! My dearest Mary … I cannot help feeling how very unfortunate we have been to be away at such a moment, and, by a fatal combination of unfortunate though unavoidable events to lose all share in the glory of a day which surpasses all which ever went before …

It was not until much later, in 1806, that he managed to get his career back on track as a result of his participation in the Battle of San Domingo during which he was involved in the capture of three prize ships. It has been estimated that these ships earned him around £1,500, enabling him to marry his fiancée, even though he was without a command for months since his ship, the *Canopus*, was sent for repairs. Losing his patron Admiral Lord Gambier in 1811 was yet another setback. Frank Austen had just been given command of the *Caledonia* but lost it when Lord Gambier was replaced a few months later. The new admiral in charge, Sir Edward Pellew, promptly gave the captaincy of the *Caledonia* to his own son-in-law. As Jane noted,

'Frank is superseded in the *Caledonia* ... Sir Edwd Pellew succeeds Lord Gambier ... and some Captain of his, succeeds Frank ... What will he do? And where will he live?'

Charles Austen faced a similar problem in 1816 as Jane Austen's niece Caroline noted in her diary:

> Feb 20: Captain Charles Austen's ship the *Phoenix* was lost. She went down – all the crew saved ... The pilot was on board. The *Phoenix* had been a lucky ship ... but her luck had now run out; perhaps she was not as se-worthy as she had been ... No blame fell on the Captain, yet such a misfortune is always a disparagement and the war being over, he knew he was likely to wait long for another ship.

The end of the Napoleonic Wars had resulted in a decrease in the size of the Royal Navy. This made it harder for officers to progress their careers, leaving many on half pay without ships. Frank Austen was one of those affected. He remained in the Royal Navy, but his lack of connections caused problems. Although he received promotions from time to time, for the next twenty-nine years he received no sea commands. As he noted, this was due purely to having 'no influence of a political or family description'. Charles Austen was given a land position dealing with coast guard operations before resuming duty at sea in 1826.

In the years that followed, both the Austen brothers used their influence and connections to help others within their families. A good example of this was Frank Austen's flagship *Vindictive* serving in North America during 1845. The officers included George (Frank's third son, as a chaplain), Herbert (his fourth son, as a flag lieutenant). He wanted to make his eldest son the flag captain but the Admiralty vetoed this appointment. He eventually promoted his son Herbert to be the commander of HMS *Vesuvius* and made his brother Charles' namesake son flag lieutenant on the *Vindictive*. In addition to the various appointments given to his sons, his daughters Cassandra and Frances came to live on board ship with him.

Prize ships were much sought after as an additional source of income. These were enemy ships and cargos that were sold by the Admiralty and the monies distributed among the crew. The sale of a captured warship could bring in £2,500. This was divided according to rank – the fleet commander gained a quarter of the available monies, three eighths went to the captain and the remainder was divided equally between other officers and crew.

Although lucrative, such prize captures could be extremely risky to achieve. In 1801, Charles Austen led four men in a small boat through a gale to capture a ship and its 149 crew members. Once on board, he held it until his own ship, the *Endymion*, could reach them. As a result, Jane wrote that he 'has received £30 for his share of the privateer and expects £10 more – but of what avail is to take the prizes if he lays out the produce in presents to his sisters. He has been buying Gold chains and Topaze crosses for us.'

It is known that during his naval career, Charles Austen was involved in capturing over twelve prize ships. He eventually became a rear admiral, Commander in Chief of the East Indies and China Station.

In addition to prize money, sailors could gain extra funds from other sources during military action. They gained £5 for each enemy killed or captured, while victorious captains received ceremonial awards of gold or silver plate. These were generally worth between £100 and £400 annually, depending on the type of ship they commanded. Annual pay for a naval captain was around £200 to £400, depending on the type of ship they commanded, but if the ship was in dock or being refitted, or if they had no ship at all, then they would only receive half pay. To make matters worse, salaries were paid up to two years in arrears.

In reality, the extra income gained by the Austen brothers as a result of prize ships and convoy costs was limited. When Frank Austen was commanding the sloop *Peterel*, he captured around forty ships but only made a few hundred pounds since most prizes were destroyed as they were 'not worth sending in'. Writing on the Jane Austen of North America website, Collins Hemingway believes that 'Tallying both his convoy fees and prize money – and allowing for other prizes we may not know about – Frank probably earned no more than £5,000 above his government pay.'

Charles Austen received even less. It has been estimated that he ultimately won around thirteen prizes, eight of which were while he was serving as a junior officer and would only have gained a small proportion of the prize money. Prizes won in Bermuda and Nova Scotia were shared with four other ships, while the solo capture of the *Nuestra* in 1806 brought him £112. He gained £540 from the capture of *Estelle* in 1808. Not every prize vessel resulted in money. Three seizures were ruled as being improper and the vessels returned to the owner, leaving Charles having to pay administrative costs to the Prize Court. In November 1808, he seized a French schooner and put twelve men on board to take it back to Bermuda. Unfortunately, the ship disappeared in a storm. Overall, he probably gained around £2,500 to £3,000 in prizes during his naval career.

Everything depended on luck and being in the right place at the right time. According to Sheila Johnson Kindred, author of a book on Fanny Palmer, Charles' Bermudan born wife, (*Jane Austen's Transatlantic Sister: The Life and Letters of Fanny Palmer*), the *Endymion* captured several merchant vessels after Charles had been transferred to another ship. If he had still been on the *Endymion*, he would have gained approximately £4,000 in prize money. Kindred points out that fortunes could be made, referring to a Captain Simpson who took enough treasure ships to earn £30,000 in just two years. Unfortunately, Simpson died before he could return home.

Jane Austen knew just how profitable prizes could be. Writing in *Persuasion*, she states that the key to Captain Wentworth's wealth was due to gaining command of a frigate operating in a good hunting ground around the Azores. Such a command had been due to his links with Admiral Croft, a rear admiral of Nelson's fleet, while the location meant that French vessels could easily be intercepted entering or leaving the Mediterranean. Wentworth states 'Ah! Those were pleasant days when I had the Laconia! … how fast I made money in her. A friend of mine and I had a such a lovely cruise together off the Western Islands.'

For many young men, the Army was a popular choice. Much depended on whether they could afford (or had relatives who could act on their behalf) to buy a commission in the regular Army. In the eighteenth century, Parliament had imposed 'property qualifications' on all Army commissions on the basis that only those who possessed property could be trusted to defend it. Hard cash was needed to pay for any commission, and having purchased one, men could ultimately sell it on to someone else when they chose to leave the Army. More money would also be needed to pay for promotion to higher ranks.

Henry Austen had initially wanted to join the regular Army but could not afford it. His sister Jane noted that:

> Henry is still hankering after the Regulars, and as his prospect of purchasing the adjutancy of the Oxfordshire is now over, he has got a scheme in his head about getting a lieutenancy and adjutancy in the 86th, a new-raised regiment, which he fancies will be ordered to the Cape of Good Hope. I heartily hope he will, as usual, be disappointed by this scheme.

Any officer in the regular Army could be ordered to serve overseas. For example, Colonel Brandon in *Sense and Sensibility* spent several years serving in the East Indies.

No such payments were required to serve in the Militia, although officers were supposed to show that they had land, a regular income or had the status of a gentleman. From 1793-1801 Henry Austen chose to serve as a lieutenant and later captain within the Oxfordshire Militia. He gained this rank simply because he was a gentleman, the son of a clergyman and had the right connections. Officially he was expected to provide financial guarantees totalling £2,000 for his role as Paymaster to the Regiment (part of the duties of a captain) but whether he was ever able to provide those securities is uncertain since he signed his accounts as 'Acting Paymaster'. His involvement in the Militia provided him with valuable experience and contacts enabling him to eventually resign his commission and take on a separate role as an Army agent dealing with banking and financial matters for his Militia regiment.

Militia regiments were organised by county, with all officers drawn from the county gentry. The concept of the Militia dates back to Anglo Saxon times when levies of adult males could be summoned to serve in the Army for a maximum period of forty days. During the Regency period, the common soldiers were chosen by lot or ballot from available lists of able-bodied men within an area. Since balloted men could pay for someone to replace them, it usually meant that most common soldiers were poor and illiterate manual labourers. During peacetime, the Militia had to drill regularly, while in wartime they were moved from their home counties to serve elsewhere. They were effectively a form of home guard, defending against foreign invasion and could not be asked to serve overseas, although Militia regiments could also be asked to volunteer for service elsewhere, such as in Ireland.

According to John Breihan's account of Jane Austen and the Militia, Militia regiments would be sent to winter quarters in inland towns such as the fictitious Meryton in *Pride and Prejudice*. The officers would be welcomed in local society, attending balls and other social events. As indicted in the novel, many of the soldiers and officers had to be found winter quarters if there were no barracks available. Local dignitaries like Sir William Lucas would be responsible for such organisation, as well as dealing with any disputes that arose. Discipline could be harsh, and usually involved flogging, with Lydia telling her sisters following a visit to Meryton that 'a private had been flogged'. In 1795, Henry Austen's Oxfordshire regiment rioted in Brighton due to accommodation problems resulting in floggings and executions.

The Church was a popular option for many young men possessing few other prospects. This required attendance at university. After gaining an initial degree, they could continue studying for higher degrees in the knowledge this would ultimately lead to ordination if they wanted to continue their academic studies. Once ordained, if they were lucky they might be able to remain at university, but to do this, according to the regulations, they would never be able to marry. The alternative was to obtain a living, which was not always easy. Parishioners had no choice as to who was appointed priest in charge of a church. Often these would be absentees, appointing a curate at a low wage to act on their behalf. As with most aspects of Georgian life, it was a matter of patronage and having the right connections. Jane's father gained his initial living at Deane in 1764 when his uncle Francis purchased it for him. His cousin, Mr Knight, gave him the more profitable living at Steventon.

Becoming a member of the clergy, possessing the status of a gentleman, did not mean being wealthy. Despite having spent time teaching at Oxford University, and then taking his first living, George Austen was not a wealthy man. When he took on Steventon, he spent over £250 just to bring the rectory to a habitable standard, which represented almost a year's income. On retiring to Bath many years later, he had an income of just £600 per year, based on his ministerial annuity.

In 1797, Cassandra Austen became engaged to the Reverend Thomas Fowle, but the couple could not marry due to lack of money. Although Tom Fowle's cousin, Lord Craven, had made him his domestic chaplain, with the living of Allington in Wiltshire, it did not provide sufficient income. When the Reverend Austen retired in 1800, he simply transferred the living at Steventon to his eldest son, James.

Other sons turned to the professions, such as law and banking. A legal career tended to be the more popular as it held more prestige. It could also generate a good income. Orphaned at an early age, George Austen owed his education and ultimate career in the Church to the help given by his rich, entrepreneurial uncle who was a practising lawyer in Sevenoaks. 'Old Francis' Austen, as he was known, is said to have used £800 gained through his work as a lawyer, as well as marrying two wealthy wives, to develop a 'large fortune living most hospitably, and buying up all the valuable land in Sevenoaks'.

After serving in the Militia, Henry advanced his career by turning to banking. This move into business initially proved very successful, allowing him to act as a bank alongside other ex-officers. Henry made a secret agreement with Captain Charles James to profit from speculation in Army commission brokerage and the agency of half pay. It was a link that also provided a way for Jane to get her books into print via his connection with Thomas Egerton, bookseller to the Ordinance Military Library. Unfortunately this link with Captain James as his silent banking partner also led to Henry's downfall. Captain James was the financial agent of Lord Moira, whose financial affairs became ever more disastrous due to Moira's level of expenditure. Henry loaned money to Lord Moira, but this was never repaid.

In 1813, Lord Moira was named Governor General of India, resulting in Henry lending a further £6,000. Ultimately this association caused major problems for Henry Austen since Lord Moira never repaid any of the loans, using his new position in India to escape payment of numerous English debts totalling over £1m. Henry was just one of the debtors who lost money as a result. His business was also affected by the general economic situation since the end of the war coincided with a period of recession. His work as the payroll banker for the Militia decreased significantly with the onset of peace.

In addition, he had made several unwise decisions, including investing in a failed brewery, and an unsuccessful visit to France in a bid to secure Eliza's claim on the estate of her first husband. The net result of these financial difficulties, combined with the non-payment of Lord Moira's debts, led to Henry Austen being declared bankrupt in 1816. After this, he changed direction returning to his clerical studies and became a curate.

Other family members were also affected by Henry's actions: Edward lost £20,000, James Leigh-Perrot lost £10,000, while Frank and Charles lost most of their savings. Jane herself lost only £13 7s since she had chosen to invest much of the £640 she had earned through her writing in Navy Stocks, which paid 5 percent annual dividends.

One final option for young men that became increasingly popular during the eighteenth and nineteenth century was to seek opportunities overseas within British trading or colonial ventures. The main focus of such work was the East India Company, which had become the effective ruler of India. A massive business operation, it constantly needed administrators, traders, officials and men to serve in its Army. Younger sons of the aristocracy and gentry were an ideal source since they possessed what was regarded as the 'right' background, as well as being ambitious.

Gaining suitable positions was highly dependent on family connections, and patronage was important. In 1811, a key reason why General Sir George Nugent gained his position as Commander in Chief of the East India Company Army was his family connections with Lord Greville, a prominent member of London society. Nugent used his new position to further the careers of members of his own family; he took two of his nephews with him, appointing them as aides de camp.

Vast fortunes could be made in India, although it was not always legitimate. Corruption was rife and many people serving in India were seeking refuge from fines and unpaid debts elsewhere. The East India Company representative in Rungpore only stayed in India for eighteen months, but during that time he acquired enough money to be able to return to England, buy a big Essex estate and enter the House of Commons. Maria, Warren Hastings' second wife, is another example. She met Warren while travelling to India. At the time she was the wife of Baron Carl Von Imoff. After divorcing the baron as soon as she arrived in Calcutta, Maria married Hastings in 1777. She eventually became extremely wealthy, and when Hastings was impeached on corruption charges, Maria possessed a fortune of over £100,000, which in modern currency would be around £14m.

'Indian Nabobs' often encountered social difficulties on returning to England, especially if they were officials who had risen in the world and were trying to copy the aristocracy. In Samuel Foote's play *The Nabob*, Sir Matthew Mite is portrayed as offering to marry one of the daughters of Sir John and Lady Oldham, while saying he will also pay for the girl's two younger sisters to go to Calcutta or Madras and 'procure them suitable husbands'. In creating the character of Sir Matthew Mite, Samuel Foote sets out to caricature a newly rich Indian nabob trying to force his way into local society and, in doing so, proving to be an embarrassment to everyone he meets.

Opting to serve in India was not an automatic route to success for younger sons. Even simply travelling out to India was dangerous and many travellers never returned to England. However, for those possessing the right connections and surviving the countless dangers in terms of climate, illness, wars, and natural dangers like scorpions and snakes, it was a way in which they could become rich and have a good lifestyle, although it usually meant rarely returning to Britain.

Chapter 8

Family Tragedy

Although outwardly light and frivolous, Jane Austen's books contain many references to the sorrow and tragedy with which women – and men – of this period were all too familiar; death and illness were always present.

Marriage was the most desirable option for women, but their chances of enjoying a long, healthy life were remote. Research based on figures from the Office for National Statistics and known mortality figures for the period show the average adult life expectancy for both male and females was around 39-40, but if an adult survived beyond that time then another twenty years might be possible. Poverty inevitably increased the likelihood of earlier death due to lifestyle, poor food, health, disease and type of employment. Yet wealth did not guarantee a long life. For example, the risk of disease and illness was constantly present; food was often tainted; lifestyles could be hazardous; riding accidents were common; serving in the Army or Navy brought its own risk, while for married women, the risk of death during childbirth was ever present.

Upon marrying, women were expected to become pregnant as quickly as possible and produce heirs for the family. This, after all, was their main function. Pregnancy and childbirth were extremely risky as there was minimal medical care available and most women were uncertain as to exactly when their child was due.

It was the normal practice during childbirth and afterwards for new mothers to spend considerable time in bed, usually in a warm, darkened room since it was believed to be very important that the woman should not be cold. As a result, the birthing room could become stifling, but windows could not be opened.

Writing in his *Treatise on the Management of Pregnant and Lying-In Women* (1773) Doctor Charles White noted that large fires would be built up in the birthing room making the air 'foul and unfit for respiration'. He added:

> As soon as she is delivered, if she is a person in affluent circumstances, she is covered up close in the bed with additional cloaths, [*sic*] the curtains are drawn around the bed, and pinned together, every crevice in the windows and door are stopped closed, not excepting the key hole, the windows are guarded not only with shutters and curtains, but even with blankets, the more effectually to exclude the fresh air, and the good woman is not suffered to put her arm, or even her nose out of bed, for fear of catching cold.

Labour could be long and arduous. Doctors were aware of the method of undertaking caesarean sections, but this was only ever attempted if the mother was dead or dying and it was the only way to save the child. The practice of forceps delivery was introduced in 1773 but had not been widely used. In 1816, Princess Charlotte, the sole legitimate grandchild of George III and heir to the throne, died five hours after experiencing a fifty-hour labour and a still birth. Her experience led to a growth in the use of forceps deliveries since it was realised that this could have saved both the princess and her child. There was no form of pain relief available during childbirth. Medical treatment during pregnancy and afterwards generally involved purges and bloodletting, resulting in women becoming anaemic. Not surprisingly, women prayed for a quick birth.

Young, unmarried women such as Jane and Cassandra Austen would have known what to expect in the event of marriage and childbirth.

They were expected to help their sisters-in-law during childbirth and afterwards. In 1809, Jane sent a message to her brother Frank saying:

> My dearest Frank, I wish you joy
> Of Mary's safety with a boy
> Whose birth has given little pain
> Compared with that of Mary Jane.

After the birth of the child, the new mother was given tea and liquids rather than light food. Strict rest was regarded as the best way of protecting the new mother against post-natal illnesses such as milk fever, puerperal fever, thrombosis and haemorrhage. This was known as 'lying in' and could last a month to six weeks. Eventually the new mother was allowed to move from her bed to a sofa, then to a dressing room and later to go downstairs to dine. She did not leave the house for some weeks after the birth.

These were conditions that generally bred infection, making it harder to recover. There were no anaesthetics or painkillers available beyond the use of laudanum, disinfecting instruments was unheard of and there was little understanding of the importance of cleanliness and hygiene, including washing hands.

Women knew they faced a high risk of death during childbirth. Up to 20 percent of women died during childbirth, particularly due to infection. Jane helped her father fill in the register of births and deaths at Steventon and her diaries acknowledge the risks women faced, with one such entry noting that 'Mrs Coulthard and Anne, late of Manydown, are both dead, and both died in childbirth.'

Within her own family, deaths and ill health from repeated childbearing were common. Mary, the second wife of Jane's eldest brother James, died in childbirth, as did Edward Knight's wife Elizabeth. Elizabeth's death was particularly sudden, dying ten days after the birth of her eleventh child, Brooke John. It had been a quick birth, with the child being born before Cassandra or any other attendant could reach her. Elizabeth appeared to be recovering well, as did her son. Her death came as a total surprise. On 8 October 1808, Fanny Austen, Elizabeth's daughter, noted in her diary, 'Oh! The miserable events of this day! My mother, my beloved mother torn from us after eating a hearty dinner. She was taken violently ill and expired (God have mercy upon us) after half an hour!!!'

The exact cause of Elizabeth's death was uncertain. Jane wrote to Cassandra saying, 'I suppose you see the corpse? How does it appear… Was Dr Scudmore [the family physician] in the house at the time, was any application attempted, and is the seizure at all accounted for?'

In 1814, Charles Austen's wife Fanny died giving birth to her fourth child while on board his ship, HMS *Namur*. She was 24 years old. The children went to stay with Fanny's parents and her older sister Harriet. In 1820, Charles married again, choosing his former wife's sister, Harriet Palmer, a relationship that was contrary to church law. Another four children resulted from this second marriage. In 1823, Frank Austen's wife Mary died following the birth of her eleventh child. The baby survived for less than a year.

Still births and miscarriages were common. Jane noted 'Mrs Hall of Sherbourn was brought to bed yesterday of a dead child, some weeks before she expected, owing to a fright. – I suppose she happened to unawares to look at her husband.'

There was general awareness that childbearing was risky and took a toll on the health of a woman, especially when there was a constant stream of pregnancies. In 1801, the Reverend Wiggett (a contemporary of the Austens living in Hampshire) wrote to his friend Mr Chute saying that his wife 'has lately been too much of an invalid. Her complaint is general weakness, the cause of which it is not difficult to conjecture when one looks at her family.' Mrs Wiggett had borne seven children and died just ten years after getting married.

Surgeon Tysoe Hancock (the Reverend Austen's brother-in-law) was equally aware of the potential problems. He noted in his writings that 'I am certain nothing shorts a woman's days so much as her being married when too young.'

Jane herself noted that her niece Anna 'will be worn out before she is thirty'. Anna experienced poor health due to a series of difficult pregnancies and miscarriages, and at one point could not visit Jane at Chawton because it was too long a walk and she had to use a donkey carriage. Fanny, on the other hand, stayed single until she was 27 years old and enjoyed far better health, as Jane recognised, telling her in a letter that, 'by not beginning the business of Mothering quite so early in life, you will be young in Constitution, spirits, figure and countenance.'

Large families were normal. Queen Charlotte, the wife of King George III, bore fifteen children between 1762 and 1783. Both Edward Knight and his wife Elizabeth, and Frank Austen and his wife Mary, had families comprising eleven children. Thomas Papilian, a Knight family relative known to Jane, had fourteen children, while a Mrs Bantry of Gloucester was reported to be delivered of a daughter – her thirty-seventh child by the same husband. Jane noted that her acquaintance, Mrs Deeds, experienced eighteen pregnancies and commented, 'I will recommend to her and Mr D the simple regimen of separate rooms.'

Women could easily find themselves having a child almost every year. Most mothers would have up to eight children in the hope that some, at least, would survive. If girls were being continually born, then there was pressure to continue trying for a boy who could inherit the property.

Family planning was unknown, with the main options available being abstaining from sex, or using the withdrawal method. Combined with family pressure to produce heirs, this meant that the majority of married women had no choice but to become pregnant time and time again.

The sheer number of children within a family was extremely costly, especially given that most of the children would have few, if any, prospects as they reached adulthood, especially if they were girls. On hearing of the news of Henry Austen's birth in 1771, Tysoe Hancock wrote to his wife Philadelphia saying: 'That my brother and sister Austen are well, I heartily rejoice, but I cannot say that the News of the violently rapid increase of their family gives me much pleasure; especially when I consider the case of my godson who must be provided for without the least hopes of his being able to assist himself.' Tysoe expressed similar feelings to Philadelphia after hearing of the birth of Cassandra Austen: 'I fear George will find it easier to get a family than to provide for them; pray give my love to them.'

The prospect of death was never far away. Britain was a country at war, which meant that anyone serving in the armed forces, whether on land or on sea, risked life and limb constantly resulting in problems for their dependants. Jane's sister-in-law Elizabeth lost her younger brother George during naval action. George had been serving on board HMS *Canopus*, alongside Jane's brother Frank. When Frank left the ship, George stayed on board, only to be killed soon afterwards.

The death of a husband caused instant problems for those left behind. In 1805, the Reverend George Austen suffered a fever. Although he felt better the next day and went for a walk, by nightfall he had become worse and died the next morning. This had an immediate effect on the family finances as the income they had received from the living at Steventon immediately stopped. It left Mrs Austen with an income of £122 annually from her family inheritance of £3,350, which had been invested in the low yielding South Sea Company. Her daughter Cassandra received £210 interest each year from money inherited from her fiancé, Tom Fowle. A total income of just £460 a year was achieved only through the good will of Jane's brothers Edward, Henry, Frank and James. Their reduced circumstances meant that they had to quickly change lodgings and seek cheaper accommodation. As Jane pointed out, 'We are just the kind of people and party to be treated about among our relations for we cannot be supposed to be very rich.'

Family tragedy took many forms. The Georgian period was one in which awareness of mental illness become increasingly prominent, especially due to the widely reported 'madness' of King George III. In 1788-89, King George experienced his first serious attack of mental illness, with further serious incidents in 1801, 1804 and then between 1810-20. His periods of illness have been attributed to a variety of causes, including a genetic blood disease known as porphyria. Most recently, the suggestion has been made that he was suffering from bipolar disorder, and eventually fluctuating chronic mania and possible dementia. A St George's Hospital research project in 2013 involved an extensive study of thousands of letters hand-written by King George III. The researchers stated that the type of sentences being used, and the long complex word structure often involving over 400 words and just eight verbs, reflected the manic phase of bipolar disorder. The King was also known to suffer from convulsions, resulting in pages having to sit on him to keep him safely in one place. His extreme behaviour and violence often led him to being confined in a straitjacket. At one point he was treated in a private asylum in Lincolnshire, and after ultimately being confined to Kew Palace, he died in seclusion at Windsor Castle.

Treatment could exacerbate symptoms. King George III was treated with medicine containing gentian, which turns urine blue, encouraging the diagnosis of porphyria. He was also prescribed emetic tartar, frequently contaminated by arsenic to induce vomiting. A strand of hair belonging to the King was analysed in 2005 and it was reported in *The Lancet* that it contained very heavy residues of arsenic; seventeen times higher than would cause poisoning by arsenic and levels that would certainly have made him very ill. Regular bloodletting and frequent purging would not have been pleasant, and sufferers were not encouraged to undertake any exercise.

Another prominent example of madness during this period was the Earl of Portsmouth. As a 5-year-old child, he had been sent for tutoring with the Reverend Austen at Steventon. He was described as 'backward' and 'eccentric', possessing a bad stammer. Over the years, his behaviour became even more erratic and eventually gained the description of the 'Vampyre Earl' due to his addiction to drinking blood. He was eventually certified.

Depending on the extent of their behaviour, members of the aristocracy and gentry experiencing mental problems would generally be either tolerated as being eccentric or confined under the care of 'mad doctors' and 'caretakers'. People of a lower social status who had no funds at their disposal became the responsibility of the community. They might become beggars, exhibits in sideshows within country fairs or confined to poor houses. There were very few asylums or hospitals for the mentally disabled. Bedlam was the only such asylum in London, and people would visit simply to watch the erratic behaviour of its inhabitants.

The term 'madness' was used as a general description to cover almost anything from depression to mania. Traditionally mental illness was regarded as being due to one of four key reasons:

- A physical problem caused by an imbalance of the humours. The Ancient Greek doctor Hippocrates developed the theory of the humours: blood = yellow; bile = black. Bile and phlegm determined health and temperament. If any of the humours were in excess or deficit, then this affected a person's health and wellbeing. This belief was still current in the eighteenth century.
- A psychological problem due to grief or stress.
- A response to a breakdown in morals caused by licentious behaviour, drink or drugs.
- Excessive religious zeal or demonic possession.

In 1733, George Cheyne promoted a new idea about mental illness in his manuscript, *The English Malady*, which suggested that increasing urbanisation and improving living standards were actually making people weaker, thus vulnerable to depression and nervous complaints.

Women were regarded as being particularly vulnerable to hysteria. The potential causes were numerous and included stomach upsets, palpitations, sensual desire, lifestyle, anxiety, eating unwholesome foods and dejection. On hearing of Lydia's elopement in *Pride and Prejudice*, Mrs Bennett retreats to her bedroom, weeping and wailing and states, 'I am frightened out of my wits; and have such tremblings, such flutterings, all over me, such spasms in my side, and pains in my head, and such beatings at heart, that I can get no rest by night nor by day.'

Insanity was often given as a cause of suicide and the frequency of suicide during the eighteenth century resulted in England being regarded as the 'melancholy capital of Europe'. Melancholy was often regarded as being fashionable – it was difficult to be accepted as a great artist or poet without being melancholic. Doctors like Thomas Trotter, author and physician to the Grand Fleet, believed that any tendency towards music or literature encouraged melancholy. He wrote that, 'persons much attracted to musick [*sic*], as being furnished with acute nerves, and nice sensibility, and of a sedentary turn, are often harassed by these diseases.' Novels were regarded as being particularly offensive and Trotter noted that these were 'one of the greatest causes of nervous disorders' since it 'creates for itself an ideal world, on the loose descriptions of romantick [*sic*] love, that leave passion without any moral guide in the real occurrences of life.'

Ladies, too, were often described as being melancholic, while reading novels left them unprepared to deal with normal life. In novels such as *Persuasion* and *Sense and Sensibility*, women fell into a state of melancholy after losing a suitor. Becoming involved with someone of a similar temperament could prove disastrous. In *Sense and Sensibility*,

Marianne develops a relationship with John Willoughby. When he disappears and it is discovered he is already engaged to someone else, Marianne is inconsolable, saying that she only came to London 'for Willoughby's sake – and now who can care for me?' She quickly becomes more and more melancholic and hysterical. Her sister Elinor advises her to lie down:

> but no attitude could give her ease; and in restless pain of mind and body she moved from one posture to another, till, growing more and more hysterical, her sister could with difficulty keep her on the bed at all, and for some time was fearful of being constrained to call for assistance.

The resultant fever nearly kills Marianne as she withdraws into a world of melancholy and romantic misery.

By comparison, it was much more acceptable for men to suffer from melancholy. Colonel Brandon says he:

> cannot remember the time when I did not love Eliza; and my affection for her, as we grew up, was such, as, perhaps, judging from my present forlorn and cheerless gravity, you might think me incapable of having ever felt ... At seventeen she was lost to me for ever. She was married – married against her inclination to my brother.

When Elizabeth Knight died suddenly after bearing her eleventh child, Jane wrote:

> I see your mournful party in my mind's eye under every varying circumstance of the day; and in the evening especially figure to myself its sad gloom: the efforts to talk, the frequent summons to melancholy orders and cares, and poor Edward, restless

in misery, going from one room to another, and perhaps not seldom upstairs, to see all that remains of his Elizabeth.

The 'Falling Sickness' was another frequent diagnosis of mental illness. By 1772, the term epilepsy was being used and was defined as being 'a disease of the convulsive kind, returning periodically, affecting the extremities with various and irregular motions; every sense, as well as the faculties of the mind, for a certain time are altogether obliterated,' and was identified by the presence of violent convulsions, the grinding of teeth, vomiting and the livid appearance of lips from which the tongue protruded. Remedies included restraining the patient, administering potions containing mistletoe, orange tree flowers and orange tree leaves. People experiencing such symptoms were shunned and stigmatised.

Jane Austen's own family would have been all too aware of the problems caused by mental illness, as it had surfaced within the Leigh family on several occasions. In 1767, Dr John Munro, a physician at the Bethlehem hospital (Bedlam) provided medical advice to the Leigh family concerning Lord Leigh of Stoneleigh. Further bills and records indicate that Dr Munro and other doctors continued to provide advice on Edward Leigh's deteriorating mental state and provide periods of care. In 1771, Dr Francis Willis was appointed to provide constant help at a cost of £1,260 per annum. Three years later, the Lunacy Commission diagnosed Lord Leigh as a lunatic enabling trustees to take over responsibility for the estate.

Mrs Austen's brother, Thomas Leigh, was known to have possessed some form of mental disability. While exact details are not known, it is believed to have included epilepsy. Thomas had been placed with a special carer, Francis Cullum, of Monk Sherborne and stayed there for the rest of his life. In 1766, Mrs Austen gave birth to a son George, who was quickly identified as suffering from fits, and possibly having other mental and physical problems. The Reverend

Austen commented, 'We have this comfort, he cannot be a bad or a wicked child.' In December 1770, Mrs Austen wrote 'my poor little George is come to see me today. He seems pretty well, tho' he had a fit lately, it was near a twelve month since he had one before, so I was in hopes they had left him, but must not flatter myself so now.' The following year, George was sent to live with the carers responsible for his uncle Thomas in Monk Sherborne. He remained there throughout his life, becoming all but invisible to the family. After his mother's death in 1823, Edward Knight arranged funds to pay for his continued maintenance.

The arrival at Steventon of Eliza de Feuillide, daughter of the Reverend Austen's sister Philadelphia, revealed that her son Hastings also suffered from fits, and was not developing like other children. In Paula Byrne's *The Real Jane Austen*, it is noted that Jane's cousin Phylly Walter observed 'the little boy had fits, could not walk or talk. Many people say he has the appearance of a weak head; that his eyes in particular … our fears are of his being like poor George Austen … I am afraid he is already quite an idiot.' Unlike the Reverend and Mrs Austen, Eliza was determined to provide what help she could for her son and to care for him herself. She breeched him early so as to encourage him to walk, taught him his letters and encouraged him to talk.

The presence of potential genetic links to mental illness were recognised when Jane wrote a letter to a relative, Mrs Harrison, commenting that her niece, Anna, who was seeking to marry against the wishes of her family with the words 'I am afraid the Young Man has some of your Family Madness – and think she inherits more of it from her Mother's family than from ours.'

Chapter 9

A Dangerous Time to Live

Illness and death were common across all age ranges and social groups. Epidemics of illnesses like typhus, smallpox and scarlet fever could spread fast among communities living close together whether in cities, towns or villages. With no understanding of the way germs functioned, the lack of cleanliness and sanitation, as well as food contamination, meant illness was endemic.

Mortality estimates by academics and organisations such as the local population studies based on Bills of Mortality indicate that around 12–13 percent of all new-born children died within their first year of life. About one child in four died before reaching its fifth birthday. In cities the figures could be even higher. During the eighteenth century, two thirds of children born in London died before they were 5 years old. It was a situation that further lessened the mother/baby bond since it was never certain whether a child would survive, and there was an automatic acceptance that many babies would die early.

Soon after birth, the new-born child would be forcibly fed 'pap' by the midwife. This was a mixture of bread or flour soaked in milk or water. Sometimes the pap would be pre-chewed by the midwife. Along with breast milk, pap would form the main diet of the baby until weaned onto solid food.

Methods of child rearing had begun to change during Jane Austen's lifetime. Traditionally, aristocratic and gentry families had engaged wet nurses and fostered children out within a few weeks of birth. This was the practice followed by Mrs Austen. In November 1772, she wrote a letter to Mrs Walter that her 1-year-old son Henry 'is come home from nurse, and a fine stout little fellow he is, and can run anywhere, so now I have all four at home, and sometime in January I expect a fifth.'

Cassandra was born in 1773 causing Mrs Austen to write to Mrs Walter saying, 'I suckled my little girl thro' the first quarter, she has been weaned and settled at the good woman's at Deane just eight weeks; she is very healthy and lively, and put on her short petticoats to-day.'

The risk of illness was a constant problem for both children and adults. As previously discussed, Jane and Cassandra, along with their cousin Jane Cooper, were sent to school in Oxford but within months an outbreak of measles in the town had led the entire school to move to Southampton. Unfortunately, this did not prove successful. Although the children avoided catching measles, Southampton was in the grip of a typhoid epidemic; a common problem especially within urban areas in the late eighteenth century.

Spread by the faeces of the human body louse, the cramped buildings of Georgian towns and streets covered in dirt and quagmires were perfect locations for encouraging the development of typhus within the community. Children frequently shared beds in schools such as that attended by Jane Austen. Living at such close quarters made it easy for typhus-infected lice to bite person after person, spreading the disease. All three children caught typhus and it was only when Jane Cooper wrote to her mother that she and Mrs Austen discovered the school had moved, and the presence of the epidemic. Both mothers travelled to Southampton to take the children home, but sadly Mrs Cooper caught typhus and later died. Jane is also said to have nearly died from the disease and had to spend eighteen months convalescing.

Tuberculosis was also rife, spreading rapidly within crowded towns and cities, especially within slums and prisons. Anyone could catch it, especially through drinking tainted milk. Known as the white plague or

Jane Austen 1775-1816, from a sketch by her sister Cassandra. (*Mary Evans Picture Library*)

Bath Pump Room. A scene outside the old pump room with an invalid being taken to drink the waters in an engraving by an unnamed artist. (*Mary Evans Picture Library*)

Ladies in a Library, c.1825. An engraving by an unnamed artist. (*Mary Evans Picture Library*)

Tales of Wonder! James Gillray's satire on the taste for Gothic novels, 1802. (*Mary Evans Picture Library*)

The Cow Pock, or the Wonderful Effects of the New Inoculation! James Gillray's satire on vaccination and the worries that it entailed, 1802. (*Mary Evans Picture Library*)

Above: Married Life, by James Gillray. (*Mary Evans Picture Library*)

Right: Warren Hastings, Governor General of India. An engraving based on a portrait by T. Zoffany (1732-1818). (*Mary Evans Picture Library*)

The Gordon Riots showing the plundering and destruction of Newgate Prison at the hands of the No Popery Mob, engraving 1780. (*Mary Evans Picture Library*)

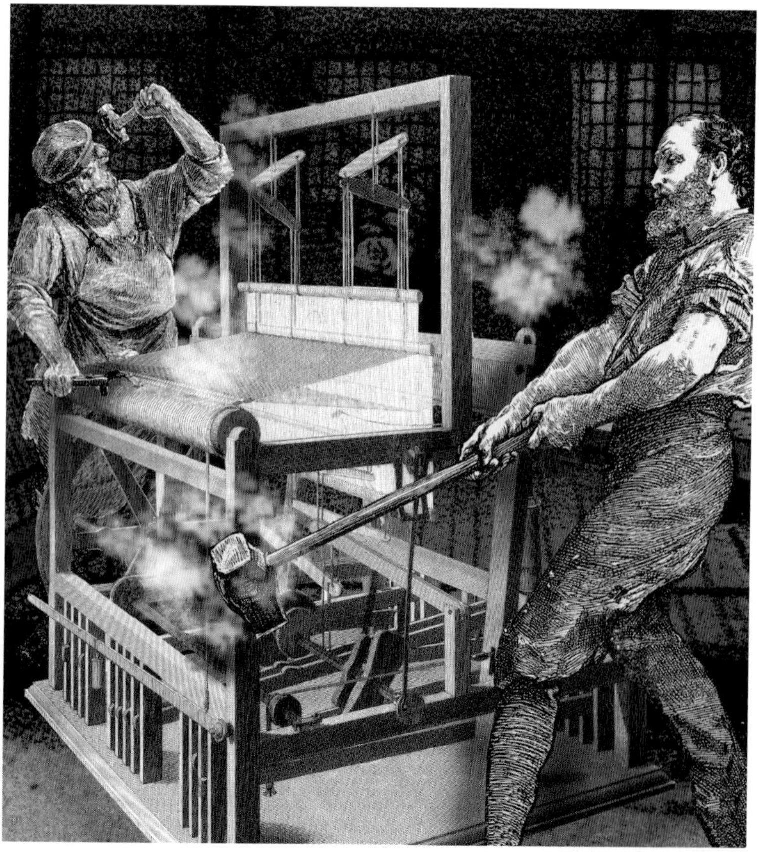

Luddites smashing weaving machinery. Engraving by Tom Gillmor, 1812. (*Mary Evans Picture Library*)

A ball in Bath Assembly Rooms, engraving 1770. (*Mary Evans Picture Library*)

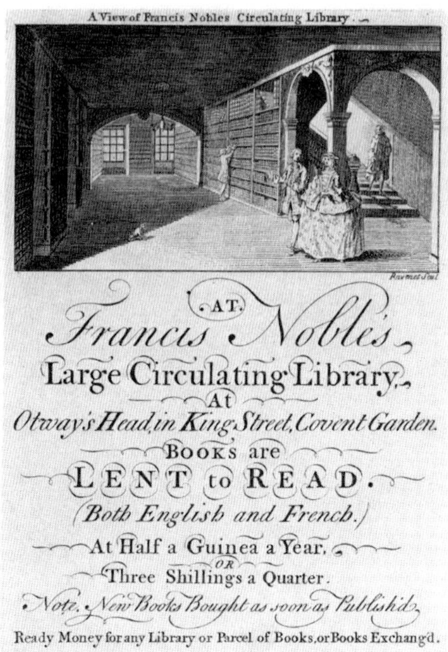

Above left: Eighteenth-century London Trade Card for Francis Noble's circulating library in Covent Garden. (*Mary Evans Picture Library*)

Above right: Josiah Wedgewood's Anti-Slavery Medallion with the inscription, 'Am I not a Man and a Brother'. The medallion became an icon for the British and American abolition movements in the late eighteenth and early nineteenth centuries. (*Mary Evans Picture Library*)

Buying laudanum and arsenic over the counter in a shop. (*Mary Evans Picture Library*)

The exterior of the Assembly Rooms, Bath, where seating identified the changing status in the marriage mart for unmarried women. (*Angela Youngman*)

The Pump Room, Bath. A popular social gathering place which Jane visited on many occasions. (*Angela Youngman*)

Taking the waters in the Pump Room at Bath. (*Angela Youngman*)

Walking by the river and shopping on Pulteney Bridge – an essential part of the social round for Georgian ladies. (*Angela Youngman*)

Stoneleigh Abbey was visited by Jane and her family when legacy hunting. (*Angela Youngman*)

Left: The story of Mr Darcy and Elizabeth Bennett continues to enthral readers. (*Karis Youngman*)

Below left: Jane Austen's novels have inspired several gothic re-imaginings, even with vampires. (*Karis Youngman*)

Below right: Jane Austen's legacy speaking to readers across the centuries. (*Karis Youngman*) scrofula, it killed around one seventh of Britain's population during the Regency period. Among the gentry, aristocracy and educated classes, it was more commonly referred to as consumption. Despite the fact it was incurable, and invariably resulted in death, being consumptive was often seen as 'romantic' due to the presence of pallid skin, and being frail, languid and the long periods required of lying in bed. To be consumptive was sometimes regarded as being creative, artistic and intellectual. Lord Byron is said to have claimed he wanted to die of consumption because it would make him interesting to the ladies.

In 1761, Warren Hastings, governor of Bengal, sent his young son George Hastings to England to be fostered and educated by Jane Austen's parents, the Reverend Austen and Cassandra Austen. A frail child, George Hastings fell ill in 1764 and died. The cause of death has been described as a 'putrid sore throat', an illness that later become known as diphtheria. This infectious disease was prevalent within eighteenth and nineteenth century society and led to numerous epidemics. It was also regarded as one of the most feared childhood diseases. There have been estimates that one in every ten children infected with diphtheria died from the disease, which included a range of symptoms from a severe sore throat to suffocation due to a 'false membrane' developing that covered the larynx, making breathing difficult.

Smallpox was another common illness of the period, despite the discovery of vaccination with cowpox as a precaution. In 1775 there was an outbreak of smallpox in the village of Enborne, Berkshire. Mary Lloyd's daughter Caroline Austen later wrote an account of how it spread within her mother's family:

> the smallpox was brought into the house by the coachman, who concealed the fact, till too late, that it was in his own cottage. My grandfather, when it broke out at the Rectory, separated himself from his family, and took lodgings … not to carry the infection into church on Sundays. The children had never been

> inoculated – I know not whether from any superstitious scruple on the part of their parents, or from a negligent delay.

All nine members of the Lloyd household were affected by the outbreak. Two of the young daughters, Mary and Martha, were both dangerously ill. Mary Lloyd (who later became Jane's sister-in-law) was left scarred for life. Mary's 7-year-old brother, Charles, died.

Vaccination with cowpox against smallpox became much more common during Jane's lifetime. Jane recorded a November day in 1800 listening to a reading of Edward Jenner's pamphlet on cowpox. According to Michael Bennett's 'Jenner's Ladies: Women and Vaccination against Smallpox in Early Nineteenth-Century Britain', Jane's friend Mrs Anne Lefoy, personally vaccinated people in her husband's parish with cowpox, noting that she had 'inoculated upwards of 800 poor with my own hands.' In 1813, Jane's niece Caroline Austen was re-vaccinated by Dr Jenner.

Epidemics of scarlet fever were not unknown. Writing in *A Treatise on Febrile Diseases* (1813) Dr Wilson Philip, physician to the Worcester Infirmary, classified scarlet fever as a contagious disease like smallpox, chickenpox, measles, the plague and nettle rash. Two versions of scarlet fever could be encountered, one being a mild fever while the other could be extremely severe with delirium and an ulcerated throat that could lead to death. Within one week in 1848, scarlet fever killed the three daughters (aged 3, 4 and 5) of Jane's nephew, the Reverend William Knight of Steventon.

Gout was a continual problem for wealthy adults, exacerbated by diets of rich sauces and dishes together with copious drinking of various liquors. An extremely painful illness, it made walking difficult. Typical symptoms included swelling around infected joints, especially the toes, which became hot and tender. Treatments included the application of electricity and drinking spa water, which is why many gout sufferers visited spa towns like Bath. In May 1799, Jane accompanied her brother Edward Knight and his wife Elizabeth to Bath, where they stayed in a house in Queen's Square. During their visit they went to the Pump Room daily so that Edward could 'drink the waters'. He also tried the new treatment of 'electricity', as Jane notes, 'he drinks at the Hetling Pump, is to bathe tomorrow, and try Electricity on Tuesday; - he proposed the latter himself to Dr Fellowes, who made no objection to it, but I fancy we are all unanimous in expecting no advantage from it.' Additional advice could be sought from a wide range of physicians. Guidebooks of the period studied by the History of Bath Research Group indicate that over thirty-one physicians, thirty-two surgeons, sixteen apothecaries, eight dentists and eight chemists could be found in Bath.

Alcoholism was common. Water was not safe to drink, which meant people opted for other liquids, especially small beers, spirits and wine. Entertaining invariably resulted in a lot of drinking, especially among the men.

Sexual diseases were rife along with the sheer number of brothels, often referred to as 'the great social evil'. James Boswell, Samuel Johnson's biographer, experienced venereal diseases nineteen times from 1760-86, according to D.W. Purdie's essay, 'The Maladies of James Boswell, Advocate'. He was not unusual. Research undertaken by the University of Cambridge highlighted in Tom Ameroth-Williams' article 'Syphilitic City' has led to estimates that over one fifth of Londoners in Regency England had contracted syphilis (the pox) by their thirty-fifth birthday, while yet more would have had other diseases like gonorrhoea and chlamydia (the clap). Most people turned to pills and potions to deal with the initial signs of a sexually transmitted illness before experiencing debilitating pain. At this point, mercury salivation was the only answer and involved at least five weeks' residential care. Treatment was available at various London hospitals, poor law infirmaries, as well as privately for those who could afford it. Many would not recover. 'A night with Venus, and a lifetime with mercury' was a popular saying of the period, which is why many aristocratic men preferred to keep a mistress. Condoms were expensive and were prone to breaking since they were handmade from sheep or goat gut.

Sea bathing was regarded as another cure-all for countless illnesses, as well as being a way of meeting potential husbands. In *The Torrington Diaries 1781-1794*, John Byng, Viscount Torrington wrote about on sea bathing at Weymouth:

> a sandy shore, being excellent for bathing, has first induced the neighbours to come; and since, by fashion, and the Duke of Glos'ters having built a house, it has become the resort of the giddy and gay; where the Irish beau, the gouty peer, and the genteel shopkeeper blend in folly and fine breeding. At these places there is ever an abundance of the fair-sex, being so well adapted for the elder ladies to get cards and company, and for the misses to procure flattery, lovers, and sometimes husbands. That the infirm, and the upstart, should resort to these fishing holes, may perhaps be accounted for; but that the healthy owners of parks, good houses, and good beds should quit them for confinement, dirt, and misery, appears to me to be downright madness.

The viscount was in a minority. Sea bathing became highly fashionable, especially after the Prince Regent decided to build a palace in Brighton. In 1783 he had been recommended by his doctors to visit Brighton and try a sea cure in order to deal with ill health, particularly gout brought on by his extravagant lifestyle. Brighton became one of his favourite places, and where he also illegally married Mrs Maria Fitzherbert. The arrival of the Prince and his entourage, plus that of other socialites, resulted in the town growing swiftly in size, and it soon become nicknamed 'London by the Sea.' From 1811-1820, the Prince Regent spent a lot of time in Brighton, either riding, promenading, entertaining and sea-dipping. Other resorts, especially along the south coast and in the south-west of England, grew rapidly. Jane Austen and her family visited these resorts on several occasions, although Weymouth was not included. She wrote to Cassandra on 14 September 1804 saying, 'Weymouth is altogether a shocking place I perceive, without recommendation of any kind, and worthy only of being frequented by the inhabitants of Gloucester. – I am really very glad we did not go there.'

Doctors of the time believed that the winter months were best to attempt health cures. Having taken her sickly son Hastings to Margate during December 1791 and January 1792, Eliza de Feuillide wrote to her cousin Philadelphia Walter: 'bathing at this time of the Year was much more efficacious than six at any other ... the sea has strengthened him wonderfully ... I still continue bathing not withstanding the severity of the weather and frost and Snow which I think somewhat courageous.'

In 1804 Jane Austen and her family visited Lyme Regis. During the visit Jane caught a fever and as part of her treatment was ordered to bathe daily in the sea. This involved the help of an assistant and Jane entered a special horse-drawn bathing machine, allowing her to change into a flannel gown in private before the machine was moved into the sea. Emerging from the bathing machine, the assistant vigorously plunged the bather into the water. Writing to Cassandra, Jane described her experience as follows: 'The Bathing was so delightful this morning and Molly so pressing with me to enjoy myself that I believe I staid in rather too long, as since the middle of the day I have felt unreasonably tired. I shall be more careful another time, and shall not bathe tomorrow.'

In *Sanditon*, one of the characters, Tom Parker, wants to develop Sanditon as a coastal resort and refers to the perceived benefits of sea bathing:

> The sea air and sea bathing together were nearly infallible, one or other of them being a match for every disorder of the stomach, the lungs or the blood. They were antispasmodic, anti-pulmonary, anti-septic, anti-bilious and anti-rheumatic ... If the sea breeze failed, the sea bath was the certain corrective, and where bathing disagreed, the sea breeze along was evidently designed by nature for the cure.

Coughs, colds and fevers were common. Jane's books often refer to an 'epidemic cold' or a 'putrid sore throat'. The most notorious example can be seen in *Pride and Prejudice*. When Jane Bennet is invited to dinner at Netherfield House, her mother is overjoyed, since it provides an opportunity for Jane to meet two eligible gentlemen. Jane's mother refuses to let her take the carriage, saying 'you must go on horseback, for it looks like rain, and then you will be forced to stay the night.' Jane does indeed get very wet and catches a cold which eventually makes her extremely ill and left bedridden at Netherfield. Mrs Bennet comments 'Oh! I am not at all afraid of her dying. People do not die of little trifling colds.'

In October 1815, Jane went to London to nurse her brother Henry who was suffering from what was described as 'a bilious attack with fever'. It was clearly more serious than initially anticipated as Jane wrote to Cassandra saying that their brother was experiencing 'a fever ... something bilious ... there is a little pain in the chest ... serious relapse' and all his siblings were warned to 'hourly expect his death'. By November he was still feverish. Among the treatments he was given were doses of barley water, stomach medicine, laxatives and he was bled by the doctor. Although he recovered in time, it left him so weak he could not initially 'hold a pen'.

Bloodletting was a common medicinal practice used for everything from headaches to gout, childbirth to fevers, the plague to smallpox. Doctors had been using this technique for thousands of years as it was believed that diseases resulted from an excess of blood in the body, thus reflecting the Theory of Humours. Treatment could involve having a vein pierced by a sharp instrument and allowing the blood to flow into a bowl. Alternatively, leeches were used. The leech was placed on the body of the patient and allowed to bite into the veins and drink until they fell off the body. One of the most well-known examples of the application of leeches was during the pregnancy of Princess Charlotte. Her death in 1817 is believed to have been exacerbated by that process, since she had been subjected to a continual course of bloodletting and starvation throughout her pregnancy, which had left her very weak.

In March 1817, Jane's 7-year-old niece Harriet (the daughter of her brother Charles) was complaining of headaches which were diagnosed as being brought on by 'water on the brain'. Jane recorded in a letter to Fanny that Harriet was treated with mercury to draw off the water since she was young enough 'not to have the Head hardened'.

Teeth are occasionally mentioned in Jane Austen's novels, with Elizabeth Bennet, Henry Crawford and Mrs Croft said to have 'tolerable' teeth. They were clearly fortunate. Personal oral hygiene during this period was minimal and generally involved the use of toothpicks. Some people used toothbrushes made with hog's hair accompanied by a paste made from charcoal, salt, brick and chalk.

Dentistry was very much in its infancy at this time. Until the mid eighteenth century, barber surgeons had been responsible for a range of treatments from pulling teeth to giving enemas. Extracting teeth involved the use of special instruments called 'pelicans' and 'keys'. The Jane Austen Centre explains how these worked:

> The pelican was a brutal instrument with a pad or bolster, which was placed on the side of the gum below the tooth to be extracted and a beak or claw which engaged the opposite side. A downward twist of the handle tore the tooth out of the mouth. The key was similar but had a handle similar to that

> of a corkscrew and enabled the instrument to be used more comfortably from the front of the mouth instead of the side.

The resultant gaps could be filled with false teeth if you had enough money. These teeth generally came from donors in need of cash and dead bodies and were placed directly into the hole left from the extraction. Given the standards of hygiene of the period, it is no surprize that there were serious infection risks associated with the practice. In 1790, London-based dentist Mr Spence published a paper entitled *Observations on a Disease Consequent to Transplanting Teeth*, which reflected on the consequences of transplanting real teeth taken from corpses (including those sourced from battlefields), as well as inserting wooden, porcelain and metal varieties.

Artificial dentures were available and might be made from wood, metal alloy, earthenware, china, cow or horse teeth and were generally ill fitting and very uncomfortable. It is known that George Washington, the first president of the United States of America, possessed a set of dentures made from whalebone and hippopotamus. Springs were attached making them somewhat uncomfortable to wear. There was also a trade in human teeth, often acquired by resurrectionists who dug up corpses. Following the Battle of Waterloo in 1815, countless dentures known as Waterloo Teeth were made from groups of teeth scavenged from dead soldiers on the battlefield.

Filing teeth was a method used to smooth out uneven teeth and was thought to prevent cavities emerging. Much depended on the skill of the practitioner as such filing could ultimately cause additional problems; too much filing could make the teeth excessively sensitive.

Visiting the dentist was a terrifying experience, especially since there was no pain relief available during treatment. In 1813, Jane wrote to Cassandra retelling the experience of taking her three Godmersham nieces to the dentist in London:

> Going to Mr Spence's was a sad Business and cost us many tears … and alas! We are to go again to-morrow. Lizzie is not finished yet. There have been no Teeth taken out however, nor will be I believe, but he finds hers in a very bad state and seems to think particularly ill of their Durableness. They have all been cleaned, hers filed, and are to be filed again. There is a sad hole between two of her front Teeth.

The following day, Jane added to her letter:

> The poor girls and their teeth! I have not mentioned them yet, but we were a whole hour at Spence's, and Lizzy's were filed and lamented over again, and poor Marianne had two taken out after all, the two just beyond the eye teeth, to make room for those in front. When her doom was fixed, Fanny, Lizzie and I walked into the next room, where we heard each of the two sharp hasty screams.

Jane also stated in her letter that 'Fanny's teeth were cleaned too – and pretty as they are, Spence found something to do to them, putting in gold and talking gravely – and making a considerable point of seeing her again before winter.' She concluded her account of the session saying that he 'must be a Lover of Teeth and Money and Mischief, to parade about Fanny's. I would not have had him look at mine for a shilling a tooth and double it. It was a disagreeable hour.'

Some improvements in dental care had begun to emerge during the early 1800s. The concept of flossing between teeth using a piece of silk thread was introduced, as were brands of tooth powder such as that patented by Mr Spence. Attention was also paid to the idea of filling cavities in the teeth. Unfortunately, the materials used probably caused even more damage to the patient's health since the filling materials ranging from tin to gold included large quantities of mercury, which could cause poisoning.

Judging by the story of Mr Spence, dentistry could be lucrative. It is believed that the dentist treating Jane Austen's nieces was George Spence, who had a business in Old Bond Street, London. He was also the dentist of King George III. In due course, he became sufficiently wealthy enough to be able to buy a country estate at Cranford. His sons did not follow him into dentistry. Instead, they were well educated and developed careers in the Church, the Royal Navy and the law.

Anyone who could not afford the fees of a dentist faced an even more daunting time; having no other option but to put up with the pain until it became too bad. At that point, people sought out a barber surgeon, a friend, or simply someone at a market or fair who was able to pull the tooth out while the person in question was held down.

Illness led to Jane's untimely, early death, although the exact diagnosis is unknown. During the last years of her life she suffered from a multitude of varying symptoms, including rheumatism, back pain, fatigue, weakness and fever. She suffered from facial neuralgia and was seen to walk with 'her head a little to one side, and sometimes a very small cushion pressed against her cheek, if she was suffering from face-ache.' On 22 May 1817 Jane wrote to her friend Anne Sharp saying, 'I have so many alleviations and comforts to bless the Almighty for! My head was always clear, and I had scarcely any pain; my chief sufferings were from feverish nights, weakness and Langour.'

Jane also complained of 'weak' eyes. She appears to have possessed three pairs of eyeglasses, which are now in the ownership of the British Library. When the eyeglasses were tested, it was discovered that each pair of glasses was stronger than the other, potentially reflecting a deterioration in her vision. No one knows whether the eyeglasses were specifically prescribed for her, or just acquired. Following the examination of the glasses, eye specialists suggested that it might reflect the presence of underlying health problems such as diabetes, which can induce cataracts. Diabetes was itself a fatal illness during the Georgian period.

Others, including academics, have suggested that Jane's illness could have been the result of Addison's disease, which is closely linked to stress. People suffering from Addison's possess adrenaline glands that do not make enough cortisol hormone to fight stress. Jane was undoubtedly under considerable stress at the end of her life as Paula Byrne points out in her book *The Real Jane Austen*, highlighting that Jane was worried over her finances and the possibility of losing their home at Chawton due to Edward Knight's inheritance problems. Byrne believes that the loss of Henry's bank led to an attack of Addison's, thus undermining her general health. The death of James Leigh-Perrot, who left nothing in his will to the Austens until his wife died, together with the fact that Edward was facing problems over his inheritance and the subsequent possibility that the Austens could well find themselves homeless, led to a further attack in March 1817, exacerbating Jane's weakness. Hodgkin's disease has also been suggested as possible alternative. This is an illness involving the white blood cells causing a cycle of illness involving fevers and night sweats, which fade away leaving the sufferer weak because so many red blood cells have been destroyed. A period of improvement follows, before a further cycle of illness begins.

Commenting on her illness to her friend Althea Bigg, Jane wrote, 'I have certainly gained strength through the Winter and am not far from being well' and that 'I am more and more convinced that Bile is at the bottom of all that I have suffered.'

The reference to bile relates to the widely held belief in the Theory of Humours, which concerned phlegm, blood, yellow bile and black bile. Jane felt that the presence of too much black bile in her body was overpowering the other humours, causing melancholy, irritability and depression. By March 1817 she was noting that she had not been well for many weeks and had been experiencing a lot of fevers and skin discolouration that later disappeared leaving her very pale.

Jane experienced a variety of treatments including bloodletting, spa water drinking and purging. Eventually she was confined to her bed and advised to travel to Winchester 'where there is a hospital and capital surgeons'. Although she travelled to Winchester, she was not admitted to hospital – this was not normal practice for people of her status in society. Jane was nursed privately close by in rented lodgings and was visited regularly by the chief surgeon, Dr Lyford. Writing to her niece Fanny in March 1817, Jane stated:

> I certainly have not been well for many weeks, and about a week ago I was very poorly, I have had a great deal of fever at times and indifferent night, but am considerably better now and recovering my looks a little, which have been bad enough, black and white and every wrong colour. I must not depend on being ever very blooming again. Sickness is a dangerous Indulgence at my time of life.

A few weeks later, in May, she wrote to Anne Sharp saying, 'my chief sufferings were from feverish nights, weakness and Languor. – This Discharge was on me for above a week.'

Over the years there have been numerous suggestions as to the cause of that final illness, including cancer, tuberculosis, lymphoma and immune deficiency. It may even have been something much simpler in the form of arsenic poisoning. A twentieth-century analysis of a lock of Jane's hair revealed that it contained large quantities of arsenic, which would certainly have made her feel unwell. Arsenic was a popular Georgian medicinal ingredient and tonics laced with the substance could bring on bilious attacks. 'Perhaps Jane, suffering from something much milder, was unintentionally poisoned by her doctors,' comments Lucy Worsley in *Jane Austen at Home*.

Food contamination and adulteration was a major problem, although awareness of the issue was little known. High taxes and poor harvests were major factors, with bad harvests in 1758 seeing alum being added to bread, and its use increased significantly over the next few years. Instances of poisoning from drinking Devon cider due to the lead content in glazed earthenware jugs are known to have occurred in 1767 and 1768, and again in 1778. There were other examples resulting from wine bottles being cleaned with lead shot.

Suggestions of contamination and adulteration problems especially in towns and cities were often regarded as something of a joke. Writing in his novel *The Expedition of Humphry Clinker*, author Tobias Smollett referred to debased London food which could include strawberries washed in spit, vegetables cooked with brass to make them green, milk in open pails through streets contaminated by splatterings from coach wheels, dirt, trash, spewings of infants, even frothed with bruised snails.

He continued, 'the bread I eat in London is a deleterious paste, mixed up with chalk, alum, and bone-ashes, insipid to the taste, and destructive to the constitution,' while 'what passes for wine among us is not the juice of the grape. It is an adulterous mixture, brewed up of nauseous ingredients, by dunces, who are bunglers in the art of poison-making.'

Deliberately adulterating food using other substances was common, as Bee Wilson points out in her book *Swindled: From Poison Sweets to Counterfeit Coffee*. She notes typical examples included Double Gloucester cheese contaminated with red lead, black pepper mixed with pepper dust swept up from the floor, linseed oil mixed with clay, cayenne pepper, sieved and rolled in oats to make little peppercorns, while fake tea was made from elder leaves, ash leaves, sloe leaves and whitethorn. Ground coffee was often thinned with chicory, roasted wheat and rye flour, burnt beans, sawdust, powder made from dried carrot or parsnips and darkened with burnt sugar. In 1818, the Attorney General prosecuted a grocer named Mr Palmer for selling adulterated tea provided by a pair of swindlers named

Proctor and Malins. They had converted various leaves by boiling, sifting, baking and rubbing to create the curled look of tea, which they then coloured with logwood from the West Indies, which in turn could cause gastroenteritis. Green tea was devised through a similar method but boiling with poisonous Verdigris and then painted with toxic Dutch clay and more Verdigris.

In 1820, an expatriate German chemist called Frederick Accum, published a book called *A Treatise on Adulterations of Food and Culinary Poisons*. Reviewing the book, the editor of the *Literary Gazette* wrote:

> One has laughed at the whimsical description of the cheats in Humphry Clinker but it is too serious for a joke to see that in almost everything which we eat or drink, we are condemned to swallow swindling, if not poison – that all the items of metropolitan, and many of country consumption, are deteriorated, deprived of nutritious properties, or rendered obnoxious to humanity, by the vile arts and merciless sophistications of their sellers.

Another reviewer in the same publication pointed out:

> Our pickles are made green by copper; our vinegar rendered sharp by sulphuric acid; our cream composed of rice powder or arrow root in bad milk, our comfits mixed of sugar, starch and clay, and coloured with preparations of copper and lead; our catsup often formed of the dregs of distilled vinegar with decotation of the outer green husk of the walnuts, and seasons with all-spice, Cayenne, pimento, onions and common salt – or if founded on mushrooms, done with those in a putrefactive state remaining unsold at market; our mustard a compound of mustard, wheaten flower, our lemonade and our punch, to refresh or exhilarate, usually cheap tartarous acid modified for the occasion.

Even drinking tea could be hazardous. Accum noted in his book that one charwoman brought green tea from a grocer's shop and found it was a 'lively blue colour'. On giving a sample of the leaves to Accum, it was discovered that they had been coloured green with toxic copper, since copper mixed with ammonia (also known as hartshorn) turns blue. The grocer denied everything.

Merely being within a house could have long term health consequences. Traces of arsenic could be found in almost all types of products at this time including wallpaper, paints and textiles. Flock wallpapers had become increasingly popular. Made from powdered wool, a waste product of the woollen industry, the wool was shaken over a fabric containing a pre-printed design covered in varnish or size (a type of glue). The adhesives contained turpentine, which can irritate the lungs, cause headaches, dizziness and nausea. The colours of wallpaper could also prove hazardous. Wallpapers might not outwardly look as if they contained a bright green dye, but were actually coated in arsenic due to the use of arsenite in the base colour, making them highly toxic with about 2 grams of arsenic per square foot. In *Shadows from the Walls of Death*, Kedzie writes:

> There is not in commerce a green paint so beautiful and unfading as the aceto-arsenite of copper. When mixed with other colours in toning it still gives a very clear and fresh colour … It is often used to give a delicacy to the shading where the unpractised eye would fail to detect any shade of green.

Bright colours were very popular in clothing and within the household. In 1778, a chemist devised a brilliant green colour known as Scheele's Green, which combined copper oxide, arsenic trioxide and water to create copper arsenite. Cheap to make, it was produced in vast quantities and used as a food colouring, as well as on numerous household items. Another arsenical green was developed in 1800 and had become widely available under varying names such as Paris Green and Emerald Green by 1814. Their popularity was undeniable, as they could be mixed with other shades to tone large areas.

Perhaps not surprising given the frequency of illnesses, food contamination, general hazards, and social and political problems, hypochondria was a common ailment in Georgian England. It had been recognised as a medical condition, generally regarded as being related to melancholy or depression and linked to the theory of humours. Writing in *Hypochondriasis: A Practical Treatise* (1764), Dr Hill described it as a 'real, and a sad disease, an obstruction of the spleen by thickened and distempered blood.' Some years later, in *A Treatise on Hysterical and Hypochondriacal Diseases* (1777), Dr Cullen, physician to the King in Scotland, listed hypochondria as a disease consisting in a weakness, often called 'vapours or low spirits'. He believed that people suffering from hypochondria were convinced that every slight change in their health could lead to danger or death.

In December 1798, Jane Austen wrote to her sister commenting 'My mother continues hearty; her appetite and nights are very good, but she sometimes complains of an asthma, a dropsy, water in her chest, and a liver disorder.' All of these were typical symptoms referred to by hypochondriacs.

Treatment for hypochondria varied but focused around the need for sufferers to seek alternative distractions. In his treatise on hysterical and hypochondriacal diseases, Dr Cullen advocated drinking mineral waters on the basis that it brought success due to the 'amusement and exercise usually accompanying the use of these waters, rather than to the tonic power of the small quantity of iron which they contain.' Other suitable distractions included exercise, un-stressful work, sports, hunting and social gatherings.

Hypochondriacs appear in several of Jane Austen's novels. The most well-known is Mrs Bennet, in *Pride and Prejudice*, who declares that: 'People who suffer as I do from nervous complaints can have no great inclination for talking. Nobody can tell what I suffer! But it is always so. Those who do not complain are never pitied.' Her illness after Lydia's elopement disappears instantly the moment she hears Lydia has been found and is to be married.

In *Persuasion*, Mary Musgrove told her sister that she had written a cheerful letter because 'I made the best of it; I always do; but I was very far from well at the time; and I do not think I was ever so ill in my life as I have been all this morning – very unfit to be left alone, I am sure.'

In *Emma*, Mrs Churchill constantly claims to be ill in order to get what she wants. She calls her nephew Frank back from a visit to his father because she was 'far too unwell to do without him' and had not mentioned it before due to 'her usual unwillingness to give pain, and constant habit of never thinking of herself'. Her nerves are a continual problem, resulting in her being unable to tolerate the London noise since 'her nerves were under continual irritation and suffering'. When Frank decides to go to the village of Highbury, Mrs Churchill suddenly had a 'nervous seizure, which lasted some hours.'

In Austen's unfinished novel *Sanditon*, the Parker sisters, Diana and *Susan*, are described as 'disillusioned by conventional medicine, preferring home-made tonics or bitters.' Observers such as Charlotte believe that much of their suffering is imaginary, or that 'some natural delicacy of constitution … with an unfortunate turn for medicine, especially quack medicine' had harmed their health. They use large quantities of bottles of salts and drops and consume very limited amounts of food. Diana says that '*Susan* never eats. I never eat for about a week after a journey.'

Even travelling around the country on business or visiting friends and relatives could be dangerous. People with their own carriages would travel with outriders to increase security but would only be able to travel at around 7 miles per hour and would have to stop regularly to allow the horses to rest. Possessing a carriage was desirable but could be expensive. The Reverend Austen purchased his own carriage in 1797, but within a year it was mothballed due to the imposition of new taxes.

Hiring a post chaise tended to make journeys faster since new horses could be hired every 10 to 15 miles. Stagecoaches were fastest of all, but it was rare for gentlewomen to travel in these unless they had no other option. Such vehicles tended to be top heavy and liable to toppling over on the uneven roads. Six passengers rode inside, and as many people as could be squeezed on the roof above.

It was customary for women to be accompanied by a man on any journey, and Jane wrote about the frustration of having to wait for her father or brother to arrive: 'my father will be so good as to fetch home his prodigal Daughter from town, I hope.' Eventually, Jane increasingly travelled on her own when visiting her brothers, who would meet her in London. Travelling by stagecoach involved worry over the fact that women could encounter unwelcome attention due to them having to sit in cramped, confined quarters. On one such journey to visit her brother Henry in London, Jane wrote to Cassandra saying that, 'I had a very good journey, not crouded [*sic*], two of the three being taken up at Bentley being children, the others of a reasonable size, and they were all very quiet and civil.'

The introduction of turnpike trusts requiring vehicles to pay for the use of roads had improved the general standard of maintenance, but the risks of vehicles overturning en route, crashing or being attacked was common. In 1798, Jane Cooper, Jane Austen's cousin, was killed in a road accident on the Isle of Wight. Even travelling by horseback could lead to death. In 1804, Mrs Anne Lefoy went shopping on horseback accompanied by a servant and experienced problems with her horse, which bolted. The servant was unable to catch it, and as Anne Lefoy tried to control it, she fell off, hitting her head on the road. She died twelve hours later.

Long journeys frequently had to be broken with a stay at an inn. These could involve having to sleep in hard, damp beds and a general lack of cleanliness. There was also the risk that luggage could go astray. As we have seen, on one occasion when at the Bull and George in Dartford, Jane found her writing and dressing boxes had been accidentally placed on chaise headed for Gravesend and onward to the West Indies. These bags contained all her 'worldly wealth' and her manuscripts. Fortunately, they were rescued in time.

Highwaymen posed a continual risk to travellers. Earlier in the century, Dick Turpin was active in highway robbery between 1735 and 1737, with a series of high-profile robberies across south-east England. His notoriety meant that he eventually had to leave London for Yorkshire, where he was arrested and executed in 1739. On one occasion, Jane Austen's aunt Philadelphia and her cousin Eliza de Feuillide encountered problems travelling across Baghshot Heath – the main route between Salisbury and London. It was an area notorious for highwaymen. Mrs Austen wrote that:

> [She] set out in a Post Chaise with only her little Bessie … In the middle of Bagshot Heath the Postillion discovered She had dropped the Trunk from the Chaise. She immediately sent him back with the horses to find it, intending to sit in the Chaise till he returned, but was soon out of patience and began to be very much frightened, so began her Walk to the Golden Farmer about two miles off, where she arrived half dead with fatigue, it being in the middle of a very hot day.

Some years later, Eliza de Feuillide referred to almost being attacked by highwaymen while travelling across Hounslow Heath on the edge of London.

Highwaymen were even encountered close to Steventon. In 1793, one of Jane's acquaintances, Wither Bramston, was stopped by highwaymen at around 10pm. Writing about the experience, he said:

> I have been very much frightened lately, by being Stopd [*sic*] returning from drinking tea with Mrs Lefroy, by a footpad,

> who put his pistol Close to me and said he would blow out my Brains if I did not give him my Money. I lost 8 Guineas which I did not like at all, besides its having made my head Ache ever since and I now Start at my own Shadow but am getting better.

War, too, caused problems, especially with regard to family life. Quite apart from the constant risk of death and injury in the wars with France, families were often separated for long periods. This could create financial problems for some, while the uncertainty of never knowing exactly when or where you might see a husband again added to the stress. In *Persuasion*, Captain Harville points out the problems for a naval family, highlighting the sailor's feelings on leaving his family and knowing that he might not return at all:

> If I could but make you comprehend what a man suffers when he takes a last look at his wife and children, and watches the boat that he has sent them off in, as long as it is in sight, and then turns away and says, 'God knows whether we ever meet again!'

Captain Harville then highlights the problems when the ship returns to port, when the sailor is looking forward to meeting his family again, but never knowing when or where this will be:

> And then, if I could convey to you the glow of his soul when he does see them again; when, coming back after a twelvemonth's absence perhaps, and obliged to put into another port, he calculates how soon it might be possible to get them there, pretending to deceive himself and saying, 'They cannot be here till such a day,' but all the while hoping for them twelve hours sooner, and seeing them arrive at last, as if Heaven had given them wings, by many hours sooner still.'

The vagaries of wind and food stocks often meant that ships docked elsewhere than originally planned, resulting in officers having to send for their families. Jane's own family was often affected by the problems caused by extended sea duties. Just after Frank Austen's wife Mary had given birth to their first child following a difficult pregnancy, Frank had to leave her behind since he was ordered to take his ship on convoy duty lasting over a year. To save money, Charles Austen lived with his wife and children on board ship. But when his wife died, along with their new baby, following a difficult childbirth, he had to send his other three children to their grandparents since he had been ordered to undertake an extended tour of the Mediterranean.

Chapter 10

Social Discontent

Despite the frothy, light-hearted lifestyle depicted in Jane Austen's novels, in reality she was living through a very tumultuous period, with economic problems, war and social discontent very much at the forefront. From 1793-1815, England and France were at war, while from 1812-15, England was also at war with America.

The French Revolution had caused concern throughout Europe. The way in which the French peasantry and townsfolk had turned on their king, government and aristocracy, and had sent vast numbers to the guillotine, had caused fear everywhere. Newspapers covered the events in great detail and *The Times* reported that 'A ring, a watch chain, a handsome pair of buckles, a new coat, or a good pair of boots, in a word, everything which marked the appearance of a gentleman and which the mob fancied, was sure to cost the owner his life. EQUALITY was the pistol and PLUNDER the object.' Monarchs, the aristocracy, gentry and educated classes were concerned in case a similar situation occurred within their own country. Britain was no exception; the fear of invasion was all too prevalent.

Jane's own family was directly affected by the events of the French Revolution. Her cousin, Eliza de Feuillide, was married to a French count. In 1794, Jean Comte de Feuillide was condemned to death and guillotined as Prisoner No. 396. Having recently suffered a miscarriage, as well as a dose of chickenpox, Eliza sought refuge at the Steventon parsonage.

The Revolutionary War that eventually transformed into the Napoleonic War lasted from 1793 to 1815. Evidence of the war would have been all too obvious everywhere within the country. Quite apart from the calls to join the Militia, the Army or being pressed into the Navy, people would have been accustomed to seeing wounded ex-soldiers with missing limbs begging on the streets. It has been estimated that during this long war, around 311,000 soldiers were killed in fighting, while around 1 million were missing or wounded. Such figures would be equivalent to 10 percent of Britain's population at the time. The reference in *Emma* to Jane Fairfax's father 'dying in action abroad' would have been instantly understood by her readers. In *Persuasion*, Captain Harville returns home suffering from war injuries. He has only a small pension but keeps himself busy with carpentry, varnishing and making toys. In *Mansfield Park*, Fanny Price's father is a former soldier and has to self-medicate his combat wounds.

When the government called for the expansion of the Militia and a volunteer force to serve as a home force designed to defend the route to London, the Reverend Austen and his son James acted as recruiters within their local area. Jane's father brought thirty-five men from Steventon to join the volunteer force, while James recruited 100 people from various local parishes to serve in the Militia. Over in Kent, Jane's brother Edward was serving as deputy lieutenant for the county. In 1793 he helped organise its Militia, and the following year took on the role of second lieutenant (cornet) in the Wingham Yeomanry. In 1803 he served as a senior cavalry captain within the Godmersham & Molash Company of East Kent Volunteers.

Henry opted for the Militia, serving in the Oxfordshire Militia from 1793-1801. During this time, he spent part of his time away in Oxford. Consequently, he was away from his unit when the sections of the Oxfordshire Militia rioted in 1795, having been asked to restore order during a time of food riots, with mobs seizing bakeries and mills to take the food. The resultant mutiny involved over 400 men from the Oxfordshire Militia who seized flour and food, selling it at cheap prices to the rural poor. The Militia were also complaining about their own meagre rations.

The mutiny was put down ruthlessly. The Lancashire Regiment of Dragoons was ordered down to Oxfordshire to suppress the mutiny and capture the ringleaders, with the military and judicial authorities seemingly determined to make an example of them.

Ten thousand soldiers, including regiments of the Royal Artillery, Militia and other regiments in the area, as well the remainder of the Oxfordshire Militia, were ordered to Hove to witness the executions and punishments. Henry Austen was one of those Militia officers present on the occasion, having been ordered back from Oxford to take part. Two ringleaders were executed by firing squad, three people received thirty lashes each, one was ordered to be transported to Australia, one remanded in custody and two were pardoned. The aim was to make an example of the mutineers so as to reduce the possibility of other mutinies occurring.

In 1797, a French invasion force of 1,400 troops set sail from Camaret-sur-Mer to invade Britain. None of the forces was well trained, and the groups included numerous ex-prisoners released from gaol to serve in the Army. Led by William Tate, an Irish-American colonel, their orders were to land close to Bristol and destroy the city. They were then expected to march through Wales to capture Chester and Liverpool. These plans quickly descended into chaos when wind conditions meant that the ships could not land, and so they changed direction and headed for Cardigan Bay in south-west Wales. The ships arrived in Fishguard Bay on 22 February and were fired on by cannon from a nearby fort. This forced the ships to withdraw, and they sailed on until they reached a sandy beach close to the village of Llanwrda. As soon as the French forces had disembarked, the ships promptly sailed back to France, sending a despatch to the authorities in Paris that the landing had been successful.

Having looted surrounding farms and villages, taking advantage of food and wine that had recently been part of a cargo from a grounded Portuguese ship, they soon became too drunk to fight. Local women led by Jemima Nicholas, wife of a Fishguard cobbler, used pitchforks to round up a group of Frenchmen and locked them in the church. According to the surrender document signed a couple of days later, the French were overwhelmed by 'troops of the line to the number of several thousand'. In reality there were no such troops in the vicinity, and it is said that the Frenchmen were misled by the presence of large numbers of local Welsh women led by Jemima Nicholas, all wearing traditional scarlet outfits and tall black hats passing by in the distance.

Additional fortifications known as Martello towers were built along the south coast between 1805 and 1812. Locations included coastal towns in Kent such as Folkestone, as well as Portsmouth and Southampton in Hampshire. It would have been impossible to ignore their presence. These round, very prominent two storey towers stood up to 40 feet (12 metres) high and had walls measuring 8 feet (2.4 metres) thick. Garrisoned by twenty-four men and one officer, the towers were topped with an artillery battery capable of firing in a 360° circle.

Between 1806 and 1809, Jane Austen lived in a rented house in Southampton. Although guidebooks of the period refer to a 'pleasantly situated' town possessing views towards 'the water, the New Forest, and the Isle of Wight', it was also a highly fortified naval base. Jane talks of walking on the ramparts, and the streets of Southampton would have been filled with soldiers, sailors and press gangs. The building of the Martello towers in the area would inevitably have been discussed within the social circles that she inhabited.

In 1808, Frank Austen, a naval officer, was involved in convoy duty bringing home British wounded and French captives following the Battle of Vimeiro, near Lisbon during the Peninsula War. The following year Jane referred in her letters to the disastrous winter campaign under General Sir John Moore; a campaign that resulted in thousands of casualties and the need to evacuate the soldiers, many of whom were brought back to Portsmouth.

It would have been impossible for anyone to ignore the constant threat of war and its effects on society. As Collins Hemingway points out in 'How the "Long War" affected Jane Austen's Family and her Novels', published by the Jane Austen Society of North America (JASNA), in just one year from 1797 to 1798:

> There were Irish rebellions supported by attempted French invasions; these did not succeed because of a lack of coordination. There was a run on the banks, leading to failures. Conscription was technically illegal, but local parishes were required to turn out a certain number of men for the Army (balloting) and this action led to protests. Impressment into the Navy led to riots in other years, but this year, it was enlisted men in the Navy who rebelled. Poor food and pay led to the mutiny, which began in Spithead and spread to Nore before it was put down. Eventually twenty-one men were hanged.

The numerous naval and land battles during the French Wars such as Marengo, Trafalgar, Austerlitz, Borondino and Waterloo resulted in thousands of casualties. References in Jane's novels to Trafalgar and talk of injuries experienced by *Persuasion*'s Captain Harville would have been instantly understood by her readers as referring to the impact of the French Wars.

Depending on where the ships were on duty, it could take months for letters and news to arrive. Even welcoming crews home afterwards involved considerable uncertainty. The wind-powered ships could find themselves changing direction or taking refuge in a totally different port forcing families to travel long distances to be with husbands and fathers.

Paying for these wars proved extremely expensive, with the cost eventually rising to £1.66 billion. Over the period of the war, numerous taxes were imposed on a constantly increasing range of items including almanacs, bricks, candles, dice, glass, gloves, hair powder, hats, sporting horses, leather, letter franks, newspapers, perfume, ribbons, servants, gamekeepers, shooting licences, sporting dogs, wine and spirits, starch, time pieces, tobacco, windows, wallpaper and wills.

Even carriages were taxed at a rate of £8.16s for one four-wheeled carriage, £9.18s for a second carriage, and £11 for every other carriage. In December 1797, Eliza de Feuillide noted that 'these new Taxes will drive me out of London, and make me give up my Carriage.' The Reverend Austen was also affected. The same year, he had acquired a carriage complete with his family crest, but in 1798 it was put into storage due to the cost of the new taxes. Two years later, income tax was imposed for the first time.

Such high taxes invariably caused widespread discontent, especially at a time when the cost of food was also high. Soon after the war with France began, the price of wheat rose from 50 shillings a quart to 160 shillings. By 1801, the cost of a loaf of bread had risen from 6d to 1s 5d. Ordinary people were going hungry, with many having little recourse but to seek assistance from the poor houses – a fact that led to increased demands for money from the landowners and gentry paying for the operation of that service. In turn this led to attempts to reduce those costs, adding to the pressures placed on the recipients.

This was a period when harvests failed on several occasions, and the scarcity of food meant that riots often resulted. The situation was made worse by the fact that the enclosure movement was gathering pace in order to create agricultural efficiency. This meant that common lands on which labourers had pastured a few animals or grown crops were no longer available since they had been fenced off under the control of farmers and landowners. Many people, especially agricultural labourers, lost their jobs. Many headed for the cities and towns in hope of finding work, while in the countryside many poor families had to enter workhouses in order to obtain a little food. Changing farming practices affected demand for agricultural workers, especially casual labourers.

Ideas, too, caused widespread discontent, challenging previously accepted views of society. For centuries, people had worshipped within the Church of England, but during the eighteenth century, the rise of Methodism had begun to pose a major challenge, particularly among ordinary people seeking greater evidence of commitment to religious beliefs and behaviour. As a result, many people were increasingly transferring their religious loyalty to the new Methodist chapels.

Revolutionary ideas were permeating society, fuelled by the French Revolution and the writings of the Thetford-born Thomas Paine. Having left the country to travel in France and America, in 1792 Paine was convicted in his absence of the crime of seditious libel due to the way he questioned the idea of private property and organised religion. People were also questioning the nature of government, and why so few were able to make their views known at elections. Even the war itself was controversial, with Whig politicians petitioning to end it. There were rebellions in Ireland, with many of the rebels seeking help from France, although the lack of co-ordination prevented such rebellions experiencing any level of permanent success.

Laws on Habeas Corpus were suspended on occasion, and people could be convicted on the slightest matter such as putting up posters, or when a Hampshire carpenter recited doggerel leading him to be imprisoned for three years. In 1795, Whig politician Charles James Fox questioned whether 'any prudent tradesman can venture to publish anything that can in any way be disagreeable to the ministers', while Wordsworth's brother advised him to 'be cautious in writing or expressing your political opinions'.

Parliamentary elections were extremely corrupt. In the eighteenth century, only property owners could vote in elections, meaning the vast majority of the population had no rights whatsoever. Patronage and bribery dominated elections to the House of Commons. Many constituencies were actually controlled by the crown or an aristocratic patron, or were in areas that had no longer had many voters. Over fifty such seats had less than fifty voters, such as Dunwich, which had only thirty-two inhabitants returning one MP. A much-quoted example of a 'rotten borough' was Old Sarum, which covered a constituency with no inhabitants. It had originally been created in the medieval period, before the population and cathedral moved downhill to New Sarum. A contemporary description of the 1802 general election noted that there were just five electors and

> This election for the borough of Old Sarum was held in a temporary booth erected in a cornfield, under a tree which marked the former boundary of the old town, not a vestige of which has been standing in the memory of man ... The Rev Dr Skinner rose and nominated Nicholas Vansittart and Henry Alexander, Esq ... No other candidates offering ... the bailiff declared the above two gentlemen to be duly elected.

Demand for political reform of the House of Commons and the electoral system grew steadily, especially since many of the large powerful towns like Manchester had no representation at all. Politicians were satirised mercilessly in popular cartoons and caricatures by artists like James Gillray. Reform organisations such as the London Corresponding Society campaigned for change. It was felt that changing the electoral structure of the House of Commons and widening the number of people who could vote in elections would not only make government fairer, but it would also allow fairer taxation and reduce political corruption.

Agitation for parliamentary reform grew stronger and stronger. There was a growing feeling that widening the parliamentary suffrage was the only way to bring about effective reform. Instead of parliamentary decisions being made by a small handful of people, many of whom had effectively purchased their seats in Parliament, it was thought that widening the suffrage would enable it to become much more representative of the total population.

At this time, only 11 percent of adult males were able to vote. The campaign for universal male suffrage, in which all men would be able to vote, had been growing in strength, despite being continuously turned down by Parliament. Mass meetings occurred, involving huge numbers of people keen to hear speeches by orators such as Henry Hunt putting forward reasons why parliamentary reform would help deal with economic issues.

In 1819, one of the biggest such gatherings occurred at St Peter's Field in Manchester. Presided over by Henry Hunt, about 60,000 people are estimated to have attended the gathering, coming from all over the north-west of England; an area that was poverty stricken and experiencing major problems within the textile industry. Many who attended were women and children, with some having walked 30 miles or more to reach the site.

Seeing the size of the gathering, the local magistrates feared the event could become the start of an armed rebellion. They declared the meeting illegal and ordered the crowd to disperse before instructing the Manchester and Salford Yeomanry to arrest Henry Hunt. The Yeomanry charged into the crowd, knocking down a woman and killing a child before arresting Henry Hunt. The 15th Hussars were then called in to disperse the crowd. Drawing their sabres, the Hussars charged. Eighteen people died and up to 700 were injured in the resulting melee.

Riots were all too common and helped create an atmosphere of widespread fear since such events were reported in newspapers with an extensive readership. Units of the Militia or Army were frequently used to break up such gatherings. Eliza de Feuillide found herself caught up in a London riot in June 1792, when soldiers read the Riot Act, warning rioters to go home or face the consequences. During the riot, Eliza's coach was attacked and her driver injured. She wrote:

> the noise of the populace, the drawn swords and pointed bayonets of the guard, the fragments of bricks and mortar thrown on every side, one of which had nearly killed my Coachman, the firing at one end of the street, which had already begun, although in short alarmed me so much, that I really have never been well since. The confusion continued all that Day and Night and the following Day, and for those eight and forty hours, I have seen nothing but large parties of soldiers parading up and down in this street, to which Mount Street is very near, there being only Grosvenor Square between. My apprehensions have been that they would have set fire to the houses they were so bent on demolishing, and think if that was to be the case how soon in such a City as this a Fire very trifling in the beginning, might be productive of the most serious consequences.

Austen refers to such a riot in *Northanger Abbey*, when Catherine Morland tells Eleanor Tilney of 'something very shocking indeed' coming out of London. Eleanor immediately thinks of rioters leading Henry Tilney to say:

> 'My dear Eleanor, the riot is only in your own brain.' … she immediately pictured to herself a mob of three thousand men assembling in St George's Fields, the Bank attacked, the Tower threatened, the streets of London flowing with blood, a detachment of the 12th Light Dragoons … Called up from Northampton to quell the insurgents.

Such riots and disturbances were also caused by changes in the working environment. This was a period when industrialisation had begun to take place, replacing craft workers with machines that required fewer people and lower wages. The Luddites were particularly active in the textile producing areas of northern England, Derbyshire and Leicestershire. There were numerous incidents of rioters destroying machines in the hope of saving their own livelihoods. People caught were usually executed. The *Leeds Mercury* declared in December 1811 that 'the Insurrectional state to which this country has been reduced for the last month has no parallel in its history, since the troubled days of Charles the First.'

In 1816, the Spa Fields Riots involved a mob led by a radical named Arthur Thistlewood rioting in Clerkenwell and robbing a gunsmith's shop. The rioters wanted to seize the Tower of London and replace the government with a Committee of Public Safety. The arrival of military forces led to the mob's dispersal, the imprisonment of the leaders and the execution of Thistlewood.

One year later, the Prince Regent's carriage was attacked following the State Opening of Parliament. Parliament believed that a revolution was imminent and ordered the arrest of printers, writers, speakers involved in the creation of seditious material.

'I have seen, within a year, riots in the country, about corn; riots about elections; riots about workhouses; riots of colliers, riots of Wilkesites, riots of government chairmen, riots of smugglers, in which customs house officers, and excise-men have been murdered, the King's armed vessels and troops fired at,' noted an appalled Benjamin Franklin on a visit to England.

This was a period of increasing economic difficulty. The end of the Napoleonic Wars led to considerable high unemployment especially among former members of the Army and Navy. Harvests failed during the 1816 'Year without a Summer', when weather patterns around the world were unseasonably cold. Parliament had passed the Corn

Laws protecting English farmers by adding a tax on foreign imported grain. As a result, bread became extremely expensive and many areas experienced a famine. This came at a time when weavers were seeing their wages cut dramatically from 15 shillings for a six-day week to just 5 shillings for the same period of work.

Social discontent continued throughout much of the nineteenth century, particularly around changes in working practices within the manufacturing industries, the periodic famines leading to food scarcity and the continuing issue of parliamentary reform. The passing of the 1832 Parliamentary Reform Act widened the franchise and removed rotten boroughs, which made a major difference, but pressure continued to build particularly through the work of the Chartist movement in favour of universal male suffrage that would allow all men to vote.

Chapter 11

Crime and Punishment

Crime and punishment were issues with which Jane was not only familiar, but members of her family were directly involved in. Her novels and lifetime reveal an awareness of typical crimes of the period, including suicide, theft, burglary and highway robbery. Georgian England was a dangerous place in which crime rates were rising and punishments handed out rapidly. Even talking to a gypsy could be a hanging offence.

In 1751, Henry Fielding, the author and founder of the Bow Street Runners, described London's maze of streets as being a perfect hiding place for criminals. Operating from Bow Street Magistrates Court in the City of London, the Bow Street Runners were tasked with enforcing the law. Gaining a reputation for dealing effectively with all types of crime, they were generally considered to be the first British police force. Fielding's comments reflected a situation that had changed little for decades, especially at night. Well off, respectable areas could be found almost adjacent to areas of extreme poverty, while slums, in which many criminals lived, were often known as rookeries. Traditionally, it was left the Watch to keep an eye on what was happening in the streets overnight, aided by the Constable who was usually a reluctant participant being voted into office. Streets were unlit and dirty. Most cities and towns experienced similar issues, with just a few exceptions like Bath where new building resulted in wider and straighter streets, although the risks involved in going out after dark remained the same.

Ultimately, there were over 200 separate offences that were punishable by death, ranging from murder and rape to poaching and criminal damage, although there was often some reluctance to impose the death penalty. An anonymous protest published in London in 1776 (which some historians suggest might be attributed to the magistrate Sir John Fielding) commented that:

> Much has been said with great humanity and truth on the dreadful frequency of executions at Tyburn, and nothing is more evident than that they have very little effect in restraining men from committing depredations on the public … It is not so much the severity as the certainty of punishment which deters men of bad morals. He who is about to commit a robbery estimates the numbers whom the jury will not convict from a proper reluctance to hang men for a petty act of pilfering, those who escape, because no evidence but the most certain will convict for a capital offence, and laughs at the danger when there are so many chances of escaping.

In Lancashire during 1793-94, some convicted murders were hung having stolen horses or a cow, while others were imprisoned for a few months. In one case, in 1793 Joseph Gill was charged with killing his wife. Gill was fined 1s and discharged, a free man. Meanwhile, James Jackson was charged with stealing seventeen fleeces and was sentenced to fourteen years' transportation.

Imprisonment could be extremely unpleasant. In 1776, Middlesex Prison was described as housing 'vagrants and disorderly women of the very lowest and most wretched class of human beings, almost naked, with only a few filthy rags almost alive with vermin, their bodies rotting with distempter, and covered with itch, scorbutic and veneral ulcers.'

Visiting Newgate Prison, London in 1813, the Quaker prison reformer Elizabeth Fry saw several people, men and women together, awaiting execution. She wrote in her account of Newgate that one of the men 'has become quite mad, from horror of mind. A strait waistcoat … could not keep him within bounds: he had just bitten the turnkey.'

Murder was part of Georgian life. Thieves might cut your throat in a dark street, likewise housebreakers, and when travelling, highwaymen might rob and kill. In 1810, Prince Ernest, Duke of Cumberland claimed to have been attacked by a would-be killer during which his page was found with his throat cut in mysterious circumstances. The following year the story of the Ratcliffe Highway murders could be found in newspapers throughout the country. A hosier, Mr Mar, together with his wife, child and a servant were brutally murdered by housebreakers. A man named John Williams was caught for the crime but committed suicide before he could be hanged. Around 180,000 onlookers attended his funeral.

In 1811, Jane Austen was staying in London with her brother Henry and socialised with the Compte and Comtesse D'Antraigues. One year later, the couple were found murdered at their home in Barnes, Surrey having been killed by their Italian manservant, who then took his own life. Since the Compte D'Antraigues was a political intriguer and secret agent, it may well have been these activities contributed to his death.

Smuggling was another common crime during this period, mainly due to the high taxes on desirable merchandise like wine, gin, tea, silks and spirits. Fishermen and traders frequently crossed the channel to buy the merchandise and secretly unloaded them in Britain and sold them to innkeepers and gentry across a wide area. In Norfolk, Parson Woodforde noted that Andrews the Smuggler brought him a 6-pound bag of Hyson Tea, for which he was paid 10s 6d per pound. It was a lucrative trade with little opposition since each excise or customs man might be responsible for overseeing miles of coastline. In the west of England, Isaac Gulliver was regarded as being 'one of the greatest and most notorious smugglers', according to Roger Gutteridge's book on Dorset smugglers. It was a trade that had made him extremely wealthy, owning a pub jointly with his father-in-law, William Beale. Gulliver also invested money in organising carriers and outlets for his smuggled wares throughout Hampshire and Devon. It was later reported by the nineteenth-century historian George Roberts that Gulliver:

> kept forty or fifty men constantly employed who wore a kind of livery, powdered hair and smock frocks, from which they attained the name of 'White Wigs'. These men kept together and would not allow a few officers to take what they were carrying when the law was altered and seizures made from smaller parties. Gulliver amassed a large fortune and lived to a good old age. A chamber open towards the sea at the mouth of the River Lyme was in existence where the 'White Wigs' took refreshment and remained in waiting until their services were required. This was about one hundred yards from the Custom House.

One of the more unusual serious crimes common at this time was body-snatching. Medical schools needed a constant supply of bodies in order to study anatomy, and many such dissections took place in public. Executed criminals were used for such dissections. With the opening of new medical schools during the eighteenth century, supply did not meet demand, leading to dead bodies being dug up after a burial and sold to the medical schools. This task was undertaken by people called 'Resurrectionists' or body-snatchers and was extremely unpopular with the public, with participants potentially facing violent mobs. However, it was extremely lucrative for the body-snatchers. *The Times* in December 1796 carried a report of such an incident:

> Early on Tuesday Morning, some suspicion being entertained that the Pesthouse burial-ground, in Old Street Road, had been frequently violated, the parish watchmen were order to

> keep a good look out, when a hackney coach was observed, waiting near the spot. Upon the watchman's approaching it, he was assaulted, and beaten, by three men, who then made off: but afterwards, springing his rattle, the assistants took the coachman into custody, who had three sacks in his coach, two of them containing the body of a man each, and the other, three children. Several other bodies, which had been dug up for the purpose of carrying away, were found under the wall of the burying-ground: and, it is generally believed that almost all the bodies deposited therein, for 5 weeks past, have been stolen, which upon an average, must have been 15 per week. The hackney coachman, who owned he was to have had ten guineas for his night's fare, was committed to the New Prison, Clerkenwell.

Bodysnatching gangs could be extremely ruthless. If corpses were not available, it was not unknown for them to be created. The most well-known examples are Burke and Hare, who operated from 1827-28. They ran a lodging house in Edinburgh and started killing their elderly tenants and selling the bodies, before starting to prey on the poor people around them. In total, Burke and Hare are known to have murdered at least sixteen people over the course of ten months, earning between £7-10 for each body. When caught and prosecuted, Burke was sentenced to death by hanging in front of an audience of over 25,000 people and his body donated to medical research. Hare was released and escaped to England. Beyond that, no one knows for sure what happened to him, but there were rumours he was thrown into a lime quarry by an angry mob, leaving him a blind beggar.

Soon after the story of Burke and Hare broke, newspapers were filled with details of yet another group called the London Burkers, or Bethnal Street Gang, who were also committing murder in order to meet demand for corpses. So well-known were such activities that it provided inspiration for Mary Shelley to write her novel, *Frankenstein; or, The Modern Prometheus* (1818).

The gallows were a familiar sight in every town, likewise the gibbet, where bodies were left to rot into a pile of bones. Executions were usually held in public and could be noisy, riotous occasions providing free entertainment and attracting thousands of spectators. Tyburn in London was the final destination for many criminals, where up to twenty people might be executed at the same time.

In 1817, the *Liverpool Mercury* recorded the execution of a group of Luddites in Leicester. Luddites were groups of industrial workers who attacked and destroyed machines that threatened to take away their jobs. If caught, punishments were severe.

> The most melancholy spectacle ever witnessed at Leicester took place this day, in the execution of seven men under sentence of death, viz, the six Luddites, for destroying lace machines, and firing with intent to kill, in the factory of Messrs. Heathcote and Boden, at Loughborough, last June; the other for arson, or setting stacks on fire, at Newbold in the said county … As early as six o'clock in the morning they were removed, under military escort, from the jail to the new Bridewell, to be executed on the new drop. On their way, the Luddites very cheerfully sang hymns all the time they passed … Many thousands of spectators kept assembling until noon to witness this truly tragic scene, and conducted themselves in the most peaceable manner … [the Luddites] spoke to several friends in the crowd, and threw oranges to some of them, and desired to be remembered to their Nottinghamshire acquaintances.

Punishments could be severe and most took place in public. Even the theft of a piece of cloth could result in transportation to Australia on special prison ships where they would be forced to take part in hard labour. Once in Australia, most convicts did not return, usually being forbidden to do as part of their punishment. Often judges allowed people to plead guilty to a lesser offence on the basis that they would be either transported or sent to serve in the armed forces. Lesser crimes might attract fines, branding with a hot iron, prison sentences, being placed in the pillory and pelted with rotten vegetables or even whipped in public. Writing in his *Diary of a Country Parson*, the Reverend James Woodforde records one such punishment that took place in 1777:

> Robert Biggen, for stealing potatoes, was this afternoon whipped tho' the streets of Cary (Somerset) by the Hangman at the end of a cart. He was shipped from the George Inn to the Angel, from thence back through the street to the Royal Oak in South Cary and so back to the George Inn. He being an old offender there was a collection of 0.17.6 given to the Hangman to do him justice. But it was not much for all that – the Hangman was an old Man and a most villainous looking Fellow indeed.

Jane's aunt, Mrs Leigh-Perrot, found her reputation damaged and became the subject of ridicule following accusations of shoplifting. In 1799, Mrs Leigh-Perrot visited a haberdasher's shop in Bath to buy a card of black lace. She purchased the card and left the shop. Some time later, she passed by the shop again and was stopped by a salesperson accusing her of stealing an additional card of white lace. This card was subsequently found in her bag. She then went home and, three days later, was arrested for Grand Larceny due to the cost of the lace involved (it was valued at 20 shillings, the equivalent of around £68 in modern currency). This was a serious offence and could be punished by hanging or transportation. Until her trial at the Taunton Assizes, Mrs Leigh-Perrot had to stay in gaol. Hearing the news, Mrs Austen offered to send Jane and Cassandra to keep her company, but the offer was rejected. Mrs Leigh-Perrot's wealth meant she could afford to pay to stay in the gaoler's house rather than in the prison itself. Her husband accompanied her, and over the next few months organised his business affairs so that he could move to Australia with her, in the event she be found guilty.

Living in the gaoler's house was not comfortable. Mrs Leigh-Perrot's letters to her cousins refer to living in a cramped building, sharing it with the gaoler's wife and five children. There was a total lack of cleanliness. She complained that they had to endure 'Vulgarity, Dirt, Noise from Morning to Night', and that her husband, James Leigh-Perrot was 'forced to experience chimney smoke in the room, children who spilt their father's beer over him and greasy toast laid on his knee by children who didn't use plates'.

During Mrs Leigh-Perrot's trial at the Taunton Assizes, the Austen family provided what support they could. Mrs Austen again repeated her offer of sending Jane and Cassandra to support her, but this offer was rejected on the basis that 'nor could I accept the offer of my Nieces – to have two young creatures gazed at in a public court would cut one to the very heart.' Her lawyers argued that Mrs Leigh-Perrot had accidentally put the lace in her bag, and privately described her as a 'smoocher' who stole small things. Joseph Jekyll, her counsel, noted in his records that 'Mrs L-P was a kleptomaniac and that she did steal the material and probably meant to.' The trial aroused great interest and was attended by thousands of people. Despite all the evidence to the contrary, the jury acquitted her in March 1800, although James Leigh-Perrot had to pay all the trial costs and lawyers' fees totalling £2,000. Soon after the trial, Mrs Leigh-Perrot was extensively lampooned in caricatures of a parrot with a card of lace in his mouth. A pamphlet reporting the trial in complete detail was widely sold at 2s a time.

The threat of a debtor's prison was always present, no matter what your position in society. Unpaid bills could result in being incarcerated in a debtor's prison until the bills were paid – but costs rose every day you were in prison. Financial problems were often made worse by the popularity of gambling, which was regarded as a normal part of life involving all sectors of society. People would bet on anything from card games to sports such as boxing and horse racing, or even simple things like which lady might have a child first, that one person's wig is better than another, and who might outlive who. Accumulating losses as a result of such gambling debts could force people into poverty, the debtor's prison, or even force them to flee overseas. Beau Nash, a celebrated dandy and Master of Ceremonies in Bath, was just one of the many social figures to lose his fortune at the gambling tables and die in poverty.

Poaching was common. While staying with her brother Edward in Kent during August 1805, Jane wrote to Cassandra saying, 'the evil intentions of the Guards are certain'. The partridge season had just begun, and landowners anticipated that poaching would occur while the Guards Regiments were on the march. The 1st and 2nd Grenadier Guards were marching from Deal to Chatham, while the 1st Coldstream and 1st Scots Guards were marching from Chatham to Deal. If caught, penalties could be harsh because it was regarded as stealing property from the estate owner.

Edward Knight was a magistrate in Kent, responsible for hearing a variety of cases such as poaching, theft and burglary. Criminal behaviour was clearly on the increase in the area. In 1805, architect George Byfield designed new prison buildings in his classic octagonal style to replace a much smaller building at St Dunstan's. It comprised a gaol and house of correction (a workhouse) linked by the Sessions House for the East Division of the Kent Quarter Sessions. Completed in 1808 at a cost of £14,856, it initially housed forty-one men and women in different wings. The octagonal outside wall was 20 feet high. When the new prison opened, inmates from St Dunstan's were shackled together and marched to the new prison. On arrival, it was discovered that the headcount was one short – a 17-year-old thief had slipped his chains and fled on the way.

Among the prisoners housed at Canterbury gaol was Barnabas Rix, whose petition for clemency was noted in the records by W.F. Botelar, Recorder of the City of Canterbury. Rix had been convicted at the January 1808 Canterbury Quarter Sessions of stealing a piece of linen, the property of Shrubsole and James Darke, linen-drapers of Canterbury in March 1807. His initial sentence was seven years' transportation, but he had clearly been sent to a prison ship. In his grounds for clemency, it was said he possessed a previous excellent character, had served two years in a prison ship and was recommended 'by some respectable people of this County' and was 'willing to serve his Majesty in any way that he may be ordered,' by being sent to serve in the armed forces. His plea was unsuccessful.

In 1813, Jane Austen accompanied her brother Edward on one of his periodic visits to Canterbury gaol. Afterwards she wrote, 'I was gratified, and went through all the feelings which people must go through, I think, in visiting such a building'.

Committing a crime like theft, murder or poaching was not the only reason why people in Georgian times faced the risk of being imprisoned. Non-payment of debts could lead to the debtor's prison. By 1779, it was estimated that there were 2,076 people in prison for debt within England and Wales, of which ninety-two were in the Marshalsea prison, London. Prison could be a devastating experience, since it left families destitute or even having to join the debtor in prison. As a result, even children and babies might be faced with living in prison alongside people who had committed other offences.

Even travelling to London carried risks for the unwary. In 1818, a *London Guide and Strangers Safeguard against the Cheats, Swindlers and Pickpockets* was published. It highlighted a vast array of potential hazards faced by visitors such as the 'hangers on' prone to stealing baggage being unloaded from coaches.

The Austen family are known to have had criminal encounters on several occasions. Quite apart from the activities of Mrs Leigh-Perrot,

Jane's cousin Eliza had problems with highwaymen and her favourite niece, Fanny married Sir Edward Knatchbull, a baronet and politician whose family were long standing connections of the Austen family. Fanny's husband's half-brother, John Knatchbull, was the family black sheep. Born in 1793, he joined the Navy where he indulged in a variety of petty frauds. In 1824, he was tried for the theft of two sovereigns and a blank cheque. Normally this would have been enough to send him to the gallows, but instead was transported to Botany Bay, Australia. He was ordered to stay for fourteen years before being allowed back to England. By 1831 he was sentenced to death for forgery, but had his sentence commuted and sent to prison on Norfolk Island, during which time he took part in two mutinies and tried to poison his guards with arsenic. After serving his sentence he went to Sydney, where he killed a shopkeeper, Ellen Jamieson, using a tomahawk. Caught and tried, he was sent to the gallows in 1844. His execution was a public one, watched by over 10,000 people and subsequently widely reported in the newspapers.

Although crime as such does not feature strongly in any of Jane Austen's novels, there are hints of an awareness of different crimes and punishments. As a clergymen, Jane's father and brother would have played a part in dealing with local discontent. In *Pride and Prejudice*, Elizabeth observes the role undertaken by the Reverend Collins and Lady Catherine de Bourgh:

> Though this great lady was not in the commission of the peace for the county, she was a most active magistrate in her own parish, the minutest concerns of which were carried to her by Mr Collins; and whenever any of the cottagers were disposed to be quarrelsome, discontented, or too poor, she sallied forth into the village to settle their differences, silence their complaints, and scold them into harmony and plenty.

Gambling, suicide, theft and adultery were frequent occurrences within Georgian society, and as Susannah Fullerton indicates in *Jane Austen and Crime*, murder also features in Jane's writing. Initially it is used as a comic element, with no indication of repentance involved. Fullerton quotes from Jane's *Juvenila*, such as 'Letter from a Young Lady' which begins with the words 'I murdered my father … I have since murdered my mother and I am now going to murder my sister … Have forged my own will, in short there is scarcely a crime I have not committed.' In another juvenile story, the lead character Sir William Montague murders his rival in love.

As her work matures, Fullerton points to examples where Jane talks about the potential for crime. In *Persuasion*, Sir Walter Elliot believes that 'ill looking men should be knocked on the head at once', while Mrs Ferrars in *Sense and Sensibility* wants to kill off superannuated servants who cost her a lot of money each year. There is also reference to suicide, or self-murder as it was known at the time, and which was regarded as a crime. In *Sense and Sensibility*, Marianne Dashwood refuses to eat proper food and care for herself, admitting later that 'had I died it would have been self destruction'. In the same novel, Colonel Brandon becomes the only person to actually engage in criminal activity since he undertakes a duel with Willoughby saying, 'We met by appointment, he to defend, I to punish his conduct'. Duelling was forbidden and the death of one participant could result in the other person fleeing into exile.

This was a violent age, and Jane Austen and her family would have been all too aware of what was happening around them, especially when visiting towns and cities like London, Bath and Southampton. News of revolts, crimes and scandals spread quickly nationwide due to the existence of countless newspapers that were exchanged between friends and families, and easily accessible via the circulating libraries.

Crime formed one of the many elements within Jane Austen's plots, even if she never chose a prison as a location, instead preferring to focus on the way in which people were inspired to commit crime and wrong-doing and the consequent damage it caused. Fullerton believes that Austen was aware of the debates concerning the need to soften or abolish laws relating to crime, stating she reflected and commented on the Georgian criminal scene with accuracy and sharp intelligence. 'Jane Austen was not a reformer,' asserts Fullerton. 'She suggests no solution to these problems. Rather she was a highly perceptive observer of her society who commented incisively on the behaviour of men and women.

Chapter 12

Opium

In the eighteenth and nineteenth centuries, the opium trade had become big business – and Jane Austen and her family were not only involved but almost certainly accidental users of opium. Derived from a species of poppy, opium had been regarded as a painkiller and sleep enhancer for thousands of years, ever since the Ancient Egyptians. By the eighteenth century, opium was impacting all ranks of society, initially due to its medicinal use, and was inextricably entwined within the British economy, trade and industry. Opium was imported alongside other cargo by all kinds of trading vessels, especially those of the East India Company, at London docks and elsewhere around the country.

Opium had become a universal cure-all and was routinely prescribed for a vast array of ailments including whooping cough, dropsy, toothache, stomach inflammation, and the hiccups. Surgeons and dentists used it as a way of anaesthetising patients before surgery, and small cakes of opium could be purchased easily from apothecaries or at markets.

Apothecaries began including opium in various medicinal compounds such as Sydenham's Laudanum, a mixture of opium, sherry and herbs and Dalby's Carminative, a combination of rectified spirits of wine and laudanum.

Laudanum, the most popular form of the drug, usually included at least 10 percent opium alongside alcohol. It was used in all kinds of preparations including pills, lozenges, wines, syrups, tinctures, compound powders, plasters, vinegar and enemas. People made their own recipes or purchased versions from apothecaries, barbers, tobacconists, stationers or grocers in towns and cities throughout the country. Whatever the format, opium was always the active ingredient, although it was sometimes adulterated with other substances such as mercury, hashish, chloroform and belladonna.

The Historic UK website states that a typical laudanum-based cough mixture would include 2 tablespoonfuls of vinegar, 2 tablespoonfuls of treacle and 60 drops of laudanum, with patients being recommended to take one teaspoon of the mixture, morning and night.

Bottles of laudanum could be found in every doctor's bag and in every household cupboard, including those of Jane Austen's family, friends and acquaintances. In 1798, a letter from Jane to Cassandra refers to their mother's habit of using laudanum: 'My Mother has not been down at all today: the laudanum made her sleep a good deal.'

A dose of laudanum was the automatic choice for dealing with any malady from bruises, coughs and diarrhoea to rheumatism, sleeplessness, fever, hangover cures, women's troubles and childbirth, as well as a soporific for babies and children. Babies suffering from teething were given laudanum to ease the pain, or to make babies and children sleep longer. It was also very affordable; 20 to 25 drops of laudanum could be purchased for as little as a penny, making it cheaper than buying an alcoholic drink.

Many of the opium-based preparations available from apothecaries and other shops deliberately targeted women and children. Such products were promoted as 'women's friends' as a way of dealing with period pains, depression, fainting fits, hysteria and the vapours. Children were frequently given preparations containing opium, alcohol and even mercury for maladies as mundane as colic. Variations of Godfrey's Cordial (or Mother's Friend) were widely distributed both in Britain and North America. The exact origins of the cordial are unknown, but often relate to a formula created by Thomas Godfrey of Hunsden, Hertfordshire, who would later give his name to Godfrey's

Cordial. Most variations contained at least 1.25 grains of opium per ounce, but overuse is known to have caused severe illness and death.

Opium use became widespread among the educated and upper classes of society. Robert Clive, the first British Governor of Bengal (later known as Clive of India) used laudanum to ease gallstone pain and depression. In early November 1774, Clive fell ill from a common cold which got steadily worse. He travelled first to Bath to take the waters, before moving to London. By this point he was experiencing considerable pain, together with a recurrence of depression and pain from gallstones. He took large doses of opium to relieve the pain but on 22 November was found dead on the floor, having just abandoned a game of cards with his friends. Newspaper reports from the period indicate that he may have sought relief from a large dose of opium, but this had proved fatal.

The experience of taking opium was regarded as helpful to creativity, since it enhanced thoughts and concepts. The poet Samuel Taylor Coleridge wrote that his epic poem *Kubla Khan* was a direct result of taking two grains of opium, with the whole poem having occurred to him during his drug-induced sleep. Withdrawal from opium proved equally creative, as he noted in his poem *The Pains of Sleep* that he was pursued by a 'fiendish crowd/Of shapes and thoughts that tortured me.'

Writing in his dual volume, *Confessions of an Opium Eater*, in which he addressed several decades of opium use, Thomas de Quincey noted that 'wine robs a man of his self-possession, opium greatly invigorates it,' and that 'its passions exalted, spiritualised and sublimed'.

The sheer extent of opium use led, inexorably, to people becoming addicted to the substance. People experienced euphoric highs followed by deep periods of depression, slurred speech and restlessness. If they stopped using opium and laudanum-based preparations, withdrawal symptoms followed in the form of aches and cramps, nausea, vomiting and diarrhoea.

De Quincey also commented on the pains of withdrawal, referring to horrendous nightmares in which he was 'stared at, hooted at, grinned at, chattered at, by monkeys, by parakeets, by cockatoos'. The experience was so bad that he felt as if he was trapped in nightmares for thousands of years, unable to escape.

Other prominent users of opium included Charles Dickens, Elizabeth Barrett Browning, Percy Bysshe Shelley and Branwell Brontë (brother of the Brontë sisters). Elizabeth Gaskell highlighted its popularity among working classes in her book *Mary Barton*, referring to John Barton 'as he sat near the fireplace (from habit) smoking or chewing opium.'

The problems of opium use continued long into the nineteenth century, although greater awareness of the problem and its potential long-term consequences had begun to surface. In 1828, the Earl of Mar died after having been a habitual opium user for many years. Before his death, the earl had insured his life as collateral against a personal loan from a Scottish bank. When called on to fulfil the policy, the Edinburgh Life Insurance Company refused on the basis that the earl's opium use had shortened his lifespan. During the resultant court action, the implications of opium use came under scrutiny, as indicated by Barry Milligan in *Morphine Addicted Doctors: The English Opium-Eater and Embattled Medical Authority*. One of the experts called to give evidence was Dr Robert Christison who pointed out that: 'It is singular how very little is known by the medical profession of the effects of the practice of eating opium or drinking laudanum on health and longevity. Yet the habit really prevails to a very considerable extent among the lower orders and better ranks of society.'

Although the Edinburgh Life Insurance Company lost its case, people began to realise that sustained opium use in any form caused problems. There were reports that nurses caring for several babies were drugging them with laudanum-based products, while one Manchester apothecary admitted selling half a gallon of Godfrey's

Cordial together with up to 6 gallons of 'quietness' each week. In 1847, the *Northern Star and Leeds General Advertiser* reported:

> Another Victim. An inquest was held at North Marston on view of the body of Thomas Walker, aged eleven weeks; the deceased was another victim of that child-destroying narcotic, Godfrey's Cordial, which was incautiously administered by an ignorant mother to prevent its crying. Two tea-spoons of Godfrey's and a decoction of poppy heads were duly given to the unfortunate deceased, who became emaciated and ill, and on the previous morning was found dead by its mother's side. The evidence went to show that the parents had otherwise treated the child very kindly. Verdict: Natural death.

Writing in his *Hints to Mothers* (1854), Thomas Bull stated that around three quarters of all deaths from opium occurred in children under five. Overdosing was common – during a nine-hour period, four drops of laudanum were given to a 9-month-old baby.

Within the Fens there were reports of opium being routinely added to beer, and large sums of money being spent in outlets selling opium. Although the 1852 Pharmacy Act had attempted to control the sale of opium-based products so that they could only be purchased at registered chemists, in reality this had little effect since chemists could sell as much as any individual cared to buy. In 1864, Dr Hunter, an inspector employed in a Privy Council enquiry, told the Privy Council while reporting on health in rural districts that opium use was so frequent that almost every surgeon in the area commented 'there was not a labourer's house in which a bottle of opiate could be seen'.

Not only was Britain a big user of opium, it was also a major opium trader, creating vast fortunes for individuals and companies, particularly the East India Company.

Founded by Queen Elizabeth I, the East India Company had been active in overseas trade across India, China and Persia since 1600. At its peak, it was the largest business of its kind, providing investors with profits that could be as high as 30 percent and creating a massive market for items such as tea, cotton and spices.

During the eighteenth and nineteenth centuries, the Company became the effective ruler of India, possessing a private army of around 260,000 soldiers. Due to the length of time it took to get letters from Britain to a specific office in Asia, the local officials of the East India Company experienced considerable autonomy. They had their own police forces and justice systems to deal with company activities within the various Indian states. The East India Company was able to develop and extend its trading activities across the Far East, and its trading fleets were frequently shielded by ships of the Royal Navy to ensure their safety against pirates, and, when closer to British shores, against French naval vessels.

The move into large-scale opium trading developed in the late eighteenth century. A triangular trade had developed in which the East India ships took Indian cotton and British silver to China, exchanging these items for the Chinese silk, tea and porcelain sought after by British consumers. It was a trade system which was heavily weighted in favour of China since China was not interested in the type of manufactured goods produced in Britain or indeed anywhere in Europe. This made imports of Chinese products very expensive, at a time when Britain was already affected by the cost of war and experiencing considerable social discontent. The continual high levels of silver being drained from Britain in payment for Chinese goods could not be sustained, and so the East India Company set out to find a way to change this balance of trade.

The Portuguese had already discovered they could import opium from India and sell it profitably within China; a trade that was soon noticed by the East India Company. In 1750, the East India Company gained control of Bengal and Bihar, the two biggest opium growing districts of India. This enabled the Company to grow and produce opium in vast quantities, trading it as a highly desirable product to Chinese merchants rather than relying on silver to pay for Chinese trade goods. Within a short time, British shipping had achieved dominance in the Calcutta to China opium trade and the East India Company became extremely profitable. While serving as Governor of Madras, Robert Clive speculated on East India stocks enabling him to return to England with a £400,000 fortune (about £668m in modern currency) and was able to establish himself as a leading member of society and buy an estate at Claremont, Surrey, spending £31,612 (£50m) building a new house and gardens.

Warren Hastings, the Governor of Bengal, was inevitably involved in this trade. The Reverend Austen and his wife Cassandra were foster parents to Warren Hastings' son, George, while his sister Philadelphia Austen (now married to Tysoe Hancock) was having an affair with Warren Hastings. Her daughter Eliza is believed to have almost certainly been Warren Hastings' child. Named as her godfather, Warren Hastings established a large dowry for Eliza, naming the Reverend George Austen as one of the trustees. As Paula Byrne points out, money for the dowry 'came from a bond for 40,000 rupees made over to Hastings to be paid in China, which he then passed over to Eliza in English money. Sums of that kind coming from the India-China connection at this period always carry the smell of opium.'

The opium trade was growing rapidly. By 1767, the East India Company was exporting 2,000 chests of opium annually to China. Warren Hastings established the East India Company's monopoly over the production and sale of opium in Bihar in 1773. By the 1780s, contractors and growers were expected to deliver to the East India Company as much opium as could be procured 'lawfully and reasonably'. Both Warren Hastings and Tysoe Hancock were said to be involved in the trade, making it a major source of their wealth.

Further opium related links with the Austen family appeared in 1793. Tysoe Hancock created Letters of Attorney, which named the Reverend George Austen as trustee to act on behalf of Philadelphia Hancock concerning her finances, the handling of receipts from India and invoices for assignments of diamonds. The Reverend Austen benefited by receiving some renumeration for the tasks he was undertaking as a trustee. As Paula Byrne indicates, 'it is startling to suppose that Jane Austen's education and the books in her father's library, which did so much to inspire her to become a writer, may well have been funded, at least indirectly, by the opium trade.'

That same year, 1793, the East India Company gained a total monopoly over the trade, resulting in Indian poppy growers being forbidden to sell opium to any other company. The resultant scale of opium being imported into China created major social problems, turning millions of people into addicts. As a result, the Chinese Emperor banned both the production and importation of opium.

Undeterred, the East India Company licensed private traders to carry the opium from India to China. These traders anchored off the coast within international waters. Chinese smugglers would buy opium direct from the ships, before distributing it throughout the country. The traders would pass on the gold and silver they had received from the smugglers to the East India Company, who used it to purchase desirable trading goods to send back to England where they could be sold at a profit.

Protecting the East India Company fleets become even more important. In addition to the highly desirable trade goods, they were often carrying large quantities of gold and silver essential to the British economy. Royal Navy ships were increasingly ordered to undertake convoy duty, protecting the fleets en route to and from China, as well as dealing with any potential problems.

It was a duty undertaken on several occasions by Jane's brother Frank Austen. His first posting upon graduation from the Royal

Naval Academy in Portsmouth was as a midshipman on board HMS *Perseverance*, based in the East Indies, where he remained for the next five years. Upon returning to England, he eventually rose to the position of captain. In March 1807, he was placed in charge of HMS *St Albans*, accompanying the East India Company trade vessels as far as the Cape of Good Hope. The following year, his ship was ordered to St Helena to collect a convoy of ships. In return for this service, Frank Austen was well paid by the merchants. Bonuses gained through his involvement with the East India Company generally ranged between £200 to £500, plus a percentage of the value of goods delivered safely.

In 1809, Frank Austen's ship was sent out to the Far East to provide support to the East India Company fleet to China and back to Britain. As captain of HMS *St Albans*, he was the senior naval officer in Canton. In October, the Chinese governor of the Guandong Province and Canton River met with Frank Austen to discuss the possibility of British naval support against pirates. Austen told them he would need a commission from the Chinese Governor General in order to take action against Chinese subjects who had not attacked him, and so a meeting with the Governor General was requested. Austen added that 'if His Majesty's ships were to be employed, he must have liberty to place them wherever he thought proper either within or without the river.' The deal was rejected.

A few months later, Frank Austen was involved in further serious negotiations with the Chinese authorities. According to letters from Charles Austen held in The National Archives:

> On 23 January, a gang of three sailors was involved in a fight with some locals in Canton, where one Chinese man was killed. The Chinese authorities claimed that they had come from a British Naval ship and insisted the men be handed over for punishment before they would give permission for the East India fleet, with its rich cargo, to sail before the monsoon arrived. The man

> charged with investigating the murder, rescuing the fleet in time to sail safely and with preserving Anglo-Chinese trade relations, was Francis William Austen.

Frank's task was difficult, requiring considerable sensitivity and negotiating skills as well as organising an investigation to discover which sailors were responsible. He could not seek advice from London since it took six months for letters to travel between Canton and the British capital. It is clear from Frank Austen's resultant letters to the Admiralty just how much responsibility, not just for naval matters but also for diplomacy and trade, was given to British naval captains.

Frank Austen began by questioning the basis upon which the Chinese had decided a British sailor was responsible. He pointed out that unless the Chinese had a witness to the murder available for him to question, there was no proof that a sailor from a British ship was involved. As he indicated, it could well have been a sailor from one of the American ships present in the harbour.

On 12 February, Frank Austen wrote to the Emperor's Viceroy stating 'the object of the English is not to screen the guilty person. They are desirous of bringing such a person to punishment but can never admit anyone to be guilty until ample proof is produced.' His letter was returned unopened. The Chinese authorities continued to insist on 'the necessity of bringing some man forward as the criminal as a matter of form.'

An inquiry was held which revealed contradictory statements and flaws within witness statements. Frank Austen stated at the inquiry, 'of all the English Captains, only one had any of his sailors in Canton that evening and they were all locked in the English factory and not one of them had a lacquered hat.' The initial verdict was one of accidental death, and a large indemnity was paid which satisfied the Chinese authorities. Austen promised to continue investigating during the long voyage back to Britain. On 2 March 1810, the

East India Fleet, accompanied by Royal Navy support vessels, left Chinese waters.

When the fleet arrived at St Helena, more investigations took place and the logbook of the Cumberland, an East Indiaman vessel in the charge of Captain Peter Wedderburn, was examined. The logbook contained an entry indicating that on 4 February, the captain's steward was notified that three sailors from Captain Wedderburn's ship had murdered a Chinese man. John James, Thomas Matthews and John Wynn had got into a knife fight over a fake dollar bill, but denied murder. Everything else was denied. Thomas Matthews and John Wynn had come to the aid of James during the fight. Frank Austen took the three sailors on board his ship, pending further investigation when the fleet eventually arrived in England. He wrote that they 'were avowedly aroused with drink … and it is highly probable that the fatal wound was inflicted by one of them but I cannot determine how justified it was as a means of self-defence.'

The East India Company wrote to the Admiralty praising Austen's actions. He noted 'it is highly gratifying to know that my conduct is not deemed deserving of censure especially when I consider how the public service has benefited from a deviation from the letter of my orders.'

Despite the East India Company's fulsome praise, Austen still had to haggle over the amount of compensation to be paid to him for conveying their treasure safely. He had been entrusted with ninety-three chests of treasure believed to contain '470,000 Dollars or Bullion to that amount' (dollar coinage had been adopted in the Dutch East Indies and was extensively used throughout the Far East). Frank was eventually paid over £500 for escorting the convoy safely to its destination. He was also offered £1,000 freight money, which he negotiated upwards to £1,500. The modern equivalent of these sums has been estimated to be around £100,000. 'There can be no doubt that this was opium money', states Paula Byrne.

Demand for opium continued to grow both at home and in China. British domestic demand for opium for medicinal and recreational use resulted in 22,000lbs being imported in 1830. Most of this came directly from India. By 1838, smugglers working with East India Company vessels were importing 40,000 chests of opium onto the Chinese mainland, costing over 9 million ounces of silver. In 1839, Chinese opium sales were so high that it paid for the entire British trade in tea.

In 1839, Lin Zexu, the Imperial Chinese Commissioner attempted to suppress the opium trade, recognising the problems it was causing to the Chinese economy, as well as the constantly increasing number of addicts. He ordered all foreign traders to surrender their stocks of opium. Charles Elliott, British Chief Superintendent of Trade in China, was forced to hand over opium stocks in Canton for destruction.

Unwilling to lose so much revenue, the traders refused, leading to the outbreak of the First Opium War of 1839-42. Skirmishes began in November when HMS *Volage* and HMS *Hyacinth* defeated twenty-nine Chinese ships. Britain sent a naval force to support the East India Company traders and when the fleet arrived in June, it quickly captured the port of Tinghai. This was followed by other action, capturing more forts. The Chinese asked for a truce and in 1841 signed an agreement providing a permanent trading site, resulting in Hong Kong becoming a British territory. Demands for compensation with regard to the destruction of opium stocks led to further conflict, which was finally resolved in 1842 with the Treaty of Nanking. This allowed the British to 'carry on their mercantile transactions with whatever persons they please', including the opium trade, although this remained illegal in China. Reparations were paid for the destroyed opium.

In 1847, Rear Admiral Charles Austen sailed for the Far East to become Commander in Chief of the East Indies and China fleet. He took with him his wife Harriet and daughters, Cassandra, Harriet and Fanny. Also on board were other officers connected to the Austen family: Charles' son (also named Charles) and his nephew Frank Austen serving as Flag Captain, three great nephews and Tom Fowle (nephew of Cassandra Austen's late fiancé). Over the next five years, Rear Admiral Charles Austen served throughout the East Indies, eventually commanding the British forces during the Second Anglo-Burmese War. He died of cholera at Prome in 1852.

In 1856, the Second Opium War broke out following political disputes and attempts to control the opium trade. The British sent warships to the area and eventually the French, Americans and Russians became involved. In the eventual treaty bringing the war to an end, trade in opium was legalised and new trading ports were opened.

It was not just China, however, that was concerned about the scale of the opium trade. Criticism of the trade and the problems opium caused were becoming increasing common. Summing up the problem and the activities of the East India Company, William Lockhart, author of *The Medical Missionary in China: A Narrative of Twenty Years' Experience* wrote:

> On the company lies the responsibility of fostering the trade in every way possible, the revenue from this source alone, in Bengal and Bombay amounting probably to some five million sterling a year … at present, the British government holds the position of a producer and dealer in opium; a position not only anomalous, but highly derogatory to the dignity of, and which can hardly be maintained with honour to, the crown.

Chapter 13

Slavery

From the sixteenth century onwards, the Atlantic slave trade proved to be a lucrative business option that ultimately affected almost everyone from landowners to housewives. It was based on a desire to exploit the resources of the new lands discovered across the Atlantic Ocean in what became known as America and the Caribbean. Vast plantations were developed to produce sought after goods such as sugar, rum and cotton. The problem was finding a suitable workforce. Overwork and disease meant that using native labour and indentured English people proved unsuccessful, and so slaves from the African continent were seen as the solution.

Elizabethan ship owner John Hawkins laid the origins of this triangular trade network. During the 1560s he led expeditions trafficking 1,200 African slaves to America and the Caribbean. His concept was simple: he took English goods to Africa, exchanged these goods for captured slaves, which he then took to the colonies in America and the Caribbean, selling them for highly desirable cargo, especially sugar, which could be sold at a profit in England. His first such voyage proved so profitable that the cash-strapped Queen Elizabeth I became one of his sponsors on future voyages. She eventually granted him a coat of arms bearing the symbol of a bound slave.

Over the next two centuries, ship owners and merchants from ports such as Bristol and Liverpool continued this lucrative trade, as did similar fleets from countries including Spain and Portugal. Vast fortunes were created as a result, partly paying for much of the development and growth of cities like Bristol, as well as providing funds for landowners and English merchants. At its peak in the eighteenth century, approximately 74,000 slaves were being trafficked from Africa, of which around 38,000 were trafficked in English ships following the established triangle trade routes. In 1756, a newspaper, the *London Advertiser* included the following regarding the sale of slaves: 'To be sold: A Negro boy about fourteen years old ... has been used two years to all kinds of household work, and to wait at table, his price is £25.'

During the late eighteenth century, opposition to the slave trade began to grow within professional and dissenting religious groups, leading eventually to the decision to establish an organisation designed to bring about its abolition. On 22 May 1787, the Society for Effecting the Abolition of the Slave Trade was established, led by a group of Quakers and Anglicans. Thomas Clarkson and Josiah Wedgewood were among the leaders of the campaign, with Clarkson focusing on the task of gathering evidence and raising awareness. William Wilberforce MP took up the cause in Parliament.

Attempts were quickly made to begin the process of introducing laws into the Houses of Parliament. In July 1788, Sir William Dolben introduced a bill to regulate the slave trade until abolition was accomplished. Although it did eventually pass through both Houses, it encountered opposition within the House of Lords, led by James Brydges, Duke of Chandos whose second wife owned a large slave plantation in Jamaica. Jane Austen's family would have noted his opposition – Jane was a distant relation, being the great grand-niece of the first duke. Remote family branches always carefully monitored such family connections in Georgian times since it was through such links that status and future success might lie.

The Abolitionists chose to focus on abolition of the trade, rather than slavery itself, as they knew that any call for complete abolition would have been successfully opposed by plantation owners and those linked to the industry. By focusing on the trade instead it was hoped that slave owners would no longer have access to a supply of new slaves, and so would have to treat existing slaves more humanely and decrease their workload.

One of the key subjects the Abolitionists chose to highlight was the inhumane and horrific conditions on board the ships. The story of one such slave ship, the *Brook*, became a cause célèbre. Launched in 1781 in Liverpool, she ultimately made eleven such trips over the next two decades. In 1788, an engraving was published showing slaves arranged on board in accordance with official regulations as required by the Dolben Act. Slaves were chained and packed into cargo areas, with no light, no fresh air, no toilet facilities and minimal food and drink. Each male slave occupied a space of 6 feet (1.8m) by 1 foot 4 inches (0.41m), women were allotted 5 feet 10 inches (1.78m) by 1 foot 4 inches, while each child slave had 5 feet (1.5m) by 1 foot 2 inches (0.36m). Thomas Clarkson commented that 'no one saw it but he was impressed … it brought forth a tear of sympathy in behalf of the sufferers'.

Over the next few decades, people like Thomas Clarkson travelled the length and breadth of the country giving talks and raising support for abolition. The campaign also led to an early example of a successful consumer boycott for political reasons. In 1791, consumers, especially women, were encouraged not to buy or use goods such as sugar that were produced by slaves in the West Indies. Around 300,000 people boycotted West Indian sugar, ensuring the campaign against the trade in slaves was kept in the public domain and encouraged many people to sign petitions to Parliament. Another sugar boycott took place in the 1820s. As sugar consumption decreased, production of sugar became less economic and weakened support for the slave trade.

Abolition bills were introduced into Parliament on numerous occasions, sometimes being deferred to subsequent sessions. Opponents to abolition were equally vociferous, for example members of parliament for Liverpool predicted 'ruin and misery' if the slave trade was abolished since 'no less than seventy millions were mortgaged upon lands in the West Indies, all of which would be lost'. They claimed the Dolben Act had resulted in ships being laid up, seamen left unemployed and that it would eventually ruin the shipping industry. There were fears of uprisings, massacres and insurrections on islands in the West Indies.

The arguments continued. William Wilberforce highlighted arguments relating to the mistreatment of slaves due to the non-residence of owners and a reliance on agents. His writings and speeches in Parliament referred to the fact that witnesses 'had seen the slaves treated in a manner, which their owners would have resented, if they had known of it,' since agents were more interested in producing profits at as little expense as possible. The immorality of the slave trade was continually stressed and how it brought shame on a Christian nation. Clarkson noted that 'the great cause of the abolition was secretly gaining ground' and that some West Indian planters in Parliament could 'see through the mist of prejudice which had covered them'.

Jane Austen's family would certainly have been aware of the abolition movement due to the frequency with which its activities were mentioned in the newspapers and discussions among clergy. Historic England indicates that during the eighteenth century, the number of Black people within England increased significantly, with estimates of around 15,000 in London alone. These people had varied backgrounds: some were former slaves, such as those who had gained their freedom from serving in the British Army during the American War of Independence, while traders often brought back Black servants from overseas, and Black sailors were a frequent sight in ports such as London and Southampton. Some became very prominent in society, including Ignatius Sancho, who acquired considerable property in London and was painted by Thomas Gainsborough; Guinea-born Joseph Emidy became an important Cornish composer and musician and the toast of Cornish society; while Olaudah Equiano played a major role in the abolition movement. There was also a significant population of mixed-race children being sent back to England from the West Indies, such as Nathaniel Wells, Brian Mackey (a vicar in Gloucestershire), and Dido Belle, the illegitimate daughter of Lord Mansfield's nephew Captain John Lindsey and Maria Belle, an enslaved Black woman.

Dido Belle was brought up in the household of Lord Mansfield at Kenwood House, London and was the beloved companion and equal of Lord Mansfield's other adopted daughter Lady Elizabeth Murray. A painting of the two young women shows Lady Elizabeth dressed in pink satin sitting with a book, reaching out to Dido, who is dressed in white satin with a gold and blue shawl and a bejewelled turban. Dido's presence at Kenwood was not always welcomed by visitors; an American loyalist by the name of Thomas Hutchinson wrote disapprovingly of a visit to Kenwood where, 'A Black came in after dinner and sat with the ladies and after coffee, walking with the company in the gardens, one of the young ladies having her arm within the other.'

It is quite possible that Jane saw the painting and visited Kenwood on one of her many visits to London, as it was common for gentry to visit large estates for a guided tour of the property. She did, however, definitely know Lady Elizabeth Murray, Dido's adopted sister. Lady Elizabeth was married to George Finch-Hatton, owner of Eastwell Park, which was adjacent to Godmersham, the estate of Jane's brother. Jane wrote about going to dinner with Lady Elizabeth at her home in 1805 and she also met her on many other occasions. Jane would certainly have known about Dido. On the death of Lord Mansfield in 1793, Dido was given an annuity and her freedom was officially confirmed. She settled in London and married an Englishman, giving birth to three sons. She was a prominent member of society and remained close friends with Lady Elizabeth throughout her life.

Criticism of mixed marriages did arise. In 1801, Maria Edgeworth, one of the most successful novelists of the period, had to rewrite her novel *Belinda* because critics had attacked her portrayal of a marriage between two characters, one white, one Black, as being 'disgusting' and 'dangerous'.

Bristol, one of the biggest British cities to profit from the slave trade, was close to fashionable Bath, where Jane and her family made many visits. Bath attracted wealthy people keen to enjoy the entertainment, company and health benefits of the natural springs. The eighteenth century had seen Bath grow dramatically, with many of the new buildings being developed funded by Bristol merchants and investors.

Trevor Fawcett noted in his talk on 'Black People in Georgian Bath' that:

> We know that the Duke of Chandos, the architect John Wood's first patron, took a leading role in the Royal Africa Company, which controlled the shipment of many cargoes of slaves to the Caribbean. The Pulteney family, who developed Bathwick, owned large estates in America. Prestigious buildings like the Royal Crescent were financed in part by Bristol capital, which in turn must have derived from the slave trade. Beckford's Tower, built in the 1820s would not have become the conspicuous landmark on Lansdown that it did without the wealth generated by William Beckford's American slave plantations.

There were also thirty brass mills in Bath's vicinity, manufacturing and exporting brass goods for the African trade. Among the Bath residents with West Indian slave links were Edward Drax, owner of sugar plantations in Barbados, and James Plunkett, whose estate was in Jamaica. Some years earlier, in 1776, James Plunkett had included the following reference in his will: 'I give to Frederick my black servant ten pounds a year for his life and I desire he may live with my sister Margaret as long as she pleases.' By comparison, James Plunkett's will indicted that he was giving Margaret Plunkett an annuity of £1,000 annually paid out of 'all messages, lands and estates in the island of Jamaica.'

Nathaniel Wells, a JP in Monmouthshire and owner of the Piercefield estate near Chepstow, was another frequent visitor to Bath. He was of mixed African Welsh heritage since his father, Cardiff-born William Wells, had moved to St Kitts in 1749 where he became owner of three sugar plantations. Nathaniel was his only surviving son, born of an enslaved house servant Juggy, later known as Joardine Wells when granted her freedom. Sent to England for his education, Nathaniel inherited the three sugar plantations and the sum of £120,000 in 1794, the equivalent of several million pounds today. Married to a white woman, Harriet, Nathaniel purchased the very large Piercefield estate and became a country gentleman, acting as the deputy lieutenant for the county, Under Sheriff of Monmouthshire, a churchwarden, and Master of Fox Hounds. He had ten children by Harriet, then a further thirteen by his second wife. They were prominent members of society, attending balls, assemblies and dances including events in Bath. Little mention is made of his colour, except for some references in various private letters recording that a neighbour had referred to the colour of his children's skin.

Wells continued to own and manage the three West Indian plantations he had inherited on an absentee landlord basis. Two plantations were eventually sold in the 1820s, and the third in the 1830s. He did, however, encounter criticism from the Abolitionists. A treatise by James Steven highlighted the fact that of those plantations owned by Wells 'in less than 12 years, [there was] the loss of 80 out of 140 human beings in the prime of life'. He went on to say 'I have seen reports of painful imprisonments, cruel floggings. These facts must be sufficiently startling even to those who know the ordinary waste of life with which we are supplied with West Indian sugar.'

There were many Quakers living in Bath, a non-conformist religious group which had always been opposed to the slave trade, and anti-slavery speakers were welcomed. Bath citizens were active participants in meetings and petitioned MPs on the subject, while Quakers from Bath took direct action by inviting escaped American slaves to speak at their meeting house and opened 'depots' to trade in non-slave products.

Roger Holly, author of *The Anti Slavery Movement in Bath* comments:

> Bath residents demonstrated significant support for the anti-slavery movement. They invited prominent members of the anti-slavery movement into the city including William Wilberforce, Thomas Clarkson, Hannah Moore, Joseph Sturge and President Lincoln's consul, Elihu Burritt. Without doubt it was the Bath Quaker Meeting that gave enormous support to the Abolitionist movement.

Holly also points out that Thomas Clarkson 'even managed to get the usually conservative and anti-radical *Bath Chronicle* on the side of the Abolitionists.'

In 1788, both the *Bath Chronicle* and *Bath Journal* covered the Society for Effecting the Abolition of the Slave Trade's declaration to oppose the slave trade and the intention to introduce laws into Parliament. The *Chronicle* noted that 'all friends of humanity would welcome the news that the slave trade, and treatment of negroes in our West Indian Islands (which have been a disgrace in Europe) will become the subject of a Parliamentary investigation.'

Such reactions were not without opposition from the city authorities. In 1792, the Bath Corporation refused permission for the Abolitionist movement to hold meetings in the Guildhall on six occasions during March and April. The Bath Corporation was more interested in maintaining the image of the city as a fashionable health resort and did not want to upset any visitors with interests in the American and West Indian plantations.

In 1808, the Abolition of the Slave Trade Act was passed, making it illegal to engage in the slave trade within the British colonies. Ships found to be involved could suffer severe penalties of £100 per slave. That penalty had to be paid by the owners of the vessel as well as by the ship's captain and crew. In addition, the ship itself would become forfeit to the Crown, and the slaves given into British custody. Companies providing insurance cover relating to the slave trade were penalised £100 and three times the amount of the premium. Although this act ended the Atlantic trade in slaves, with no further slaves being taken from Africa to the West Indies, slavery did continue on the plantations with regard to the those who had been brought over in previous years. They were not free. As a result, the Abolitionists continued to campaign to abolish the slave trade completely. In 1823, the Anti-Slavery Society was established to implement the abolition of slavery throughout the Empire.

When the Slavery Abolition Act was finally achieved in 1833, Bath resident Hastings Elwin (1777-1852), a co-founder of the Bath Royal Literary and Scientific Institution, was appointed a commissioner for Slave Compensation. The end of slavery within British colonies was phased over six years. In total, sixty-six people in Bath applied for such compensation. Among them was Edward Drax, who lived in Queen's Parade, who received £4,239 12s 6d compensation relating to 189 slaves, the equivalent of £22 43d per slave. Nathaniel Wells was awarded £1,400 9s 7d on 13 February 1837 in compensation for eighty-six slaves on his Fahies and Ortons sugar estates on St Kitts.

Although Jane Austen rarely makes specific references to political events and issues within her novels, an exception is made for the slave trade in *Mansfield Park* and *Emma*, as well as her unfinished novel, *Sanditon*.

Mansfield Park is set in the early 1800s, when the Abolitionist movement was underway. Sir Thomas Bertram has just returned after spending two years in Antigua on urgent business. Although no indication is given as to the nature of that business, there are references to 'poor returns' and that 'a large part of his income was unsettled', implying the possibility that following the 1807 Abolition Act, his plantation was suffering from competition from foreign sugar producers who were still using slaves.

Later in the book, during a discussion with Edmund, Fanny recalls attempting to speak to her uncle who had just returned from Antigua where he operated a plantation.

> [Fanny] 'Did not you hear me ask him about the slave-trade last night?'
>
> [Edmund] 'I did – and was in hopes the question would be followed up by others. It would have pleased your uncle to be inquired of farther.'
>
> [Fanny] 'And I longed to do it – but there was such a dead silence! And while my cousins were sitting by without speaking a word, or seeming at all interested in the subject, I did not like – I thought it would appear as if I wanted to set myself off at their expense, by shewing a curiosity and pleasure in his information which he must wish his own daughters to feel.'

Among the reasons put forward for this silence from Sir Thomas' daughters include possible embarrassment at the family's involvement in the trade, the substantial potential losses amounting to several thousand pounds annually, and a general reluctance to discuss the subject.

It has been suggested the book title itself may form a link to the slave trade issue. Lord Mansfield, the guardian of Dido Belle, was a senior judge who issued a ruling on the case of James Somerset, a slave who had escaped from his master while in England. Somerset had been recaptured and was due to be sent back to the West Indies and sold. A writ of Habeas Corpus was issued, and Lord Mansfield ruled there was a case to be heard. His eventual ruling affected all slave owning families in Britain since it stated that a slave could not be returned against his will. His verdict declared: 'The state of slavery … is so odious … Whatever inconvenience, therefore, may follow from the decision, I cannot say that this case is allowed or approved by the law of England; and therefore, the black must be discharged.'

In *Emma*, the work of a governess is compared to the slave trade when Jane Fairfax comments, 'I am not at all afraid of being long unemployed. There are places in town, offices, where inquiry would soon produce something – offices for the sale, not quite of human flesh, but of human intellect.'

Responding to her comment, Mrs Elton declares:

> 'Oh! my dear, human flesh! You quite shock me; if you mean a fling at the slave-trade, I assure you Mr Suckling was always rather a friend to the abolition.'
>
> 'I did not mean, I was not thinking of the slave trade,' replied Jane, 'governess-trade, I assure you, was all that I had in view; widely different certainly as to the guilt of those who carry it on; but as to the greater misery of the victims, I do not know where it lies.'

Jane's unfinished novel, *Sanditon*, takes a different slant on the subject by presenting one of her heroines, Miss Lambe, as being of mixed-race West Indian descent and the daughter of a plantation owner. She writes:

> Miss Lambe was beyond comparison the most important and precious, as she paid in proportion to her fortune. She was about seventeen, half mulatto, chilly and tender, had a maid of her own, was to have the best room in the lodgings, and was always of the first consequence in every plan of Mrs Griffiths.

Two other English girls from the West Indies, the Miss Beauforts, travel with Miss Lambe to Sanditon. An elderly widow, Lady Denham, immediately targets Miss Lambe, regarding her as the ideal future wife for the dissolute Sir Edward Denham, Lady Denham's nephew. Money is the key attraction:

> 'No people spend more freely, I believe, than West Indians,' observed Mr Parker.
>
> [Lady Denham]: 'Aye, so I have heard, and because they have full purses fancy themselves equal, may be, to your old country families.'

As with almost all other families of similar status in England, the Austen family had links to the West Indian slave plantations. In 1760, Jane's father, the Reverend George Austen, became the principal trustee of an Antiguan sugar plantation owned by his Oxford contemporary, James Langford Nibbs, who may have been taught by George Austen. Nibbs was a member of an English family who had been sugar magnates in Antigua since 1671, and the earliest map of Antigua, produced in 1750, indicates that the Nibbs family owned an extensive network of large properties throughout the island. As the principal trustee of the plantation, as well as the co-trustee of a marriage settlement between

James Nibbs and his cousin Barbara, George Austen would have been responsible for dispersing plantation property and profits. However, he would not have been involved in directly running the plantation. The links between the James Nibbs and the Reverend Austen grew deeper over time, with Nibbs becoming godfather to James Austen, Jane's older brother. In 1801, Jane refers in her correspondence to a picture of Mr Nibbs on the wall in the Steventon Parsonage.

The Reverend Austen possessed another link to the slave trade and West Indian plantations thanks to personal connections to the Hampson and Walters families via his older half-brother by his mother, Rebecca Hampson's first husband. The Reverend Austen's stepbrother, William Hampson Walter, was part of a family that owned plantations in Jamaica and two of William's sons were sent out there. As a result, Jane Austen had a cousin called Sir Thomas, who was the owner of a slave plantation.

Other links to the West Indies came through the family of Cassandra Leigh Austen, Jane's mother. Jane's great-grandparents were Theophilus Leigh and the Hon. Mary Brydges, sister to the Duke of Chandos, whose financial interests included the shipping of African slaves to the Caribbean. The Leigh family were also linked to the Beckford family, which had created a fortune from sugar plantations in the West Indies. An absentee landowner, Alderman Beckford became Lord Mayor of London in 1762 and was nicknamed the 'uncrowned king of Jamaica', possessing over 20,000 acres, thirteen plantations and 3,000 slaves. Dissent was forcefully put down. A slave rebellion on one of his estates led to over 400 slaves being killed, and the slave leaders executed – one leader was burnt alive, while two others were hung to dry in irons. William Beckford inherited the fortune when he was only 10 years old and grew up to be more interested in art, architecture and music. An alleged sexual assault on William Courtenay, heir to Powderham Castle, Devon resulted in Beckford fleeing England for several years. On his return he rebuilt Fonthill Abbey in Wiltshire, and later constructed the 120-foot Beckford's Tower in Bath, located in a garden known as Beckford's Ride which ran from his house in Lansdown Crescent to the top of Lansdown Hill.

Cassandra's older brother James inherited a fortune from a childless relative and added his late uncle's name to his own, becoming James Leigh-Perrot. James was married to Jane Leigh-Perrot, who was heiress to a planation in Barbados. Jane Leigh-Perrot was born in the West Indies and then sent to school in England aged 6. The two families were close and in 1797 Jane Austen stayed with them in Bath as a way of meeting prospective suitors among the fashionable people visiting the city.

The Austen family also had friends who were involved in the slave trade. Brothers William and James Holder rented Ashe Park, near Steventon and often met up with the Austen family; James Holder shared his newspaper with the Austens on a regular basis.

Although direct references in her books are limited, there is no doubt Jane Austen would have been very much aware of the issues surrounding the slave trade. The sheer scale of the activities of the Society for Abolition of the Slave Trade would have been impossible to ignore. Distribution of literature was widespread and would have been accessible in homes and circulating libraries. In mid-1788, the well-known Abolitionist Thomas Clarkson claimed that 51,400 pamphlets and books had been distributed 'not at random, but judiciously, and through respectable channels'. As a clergyman, Clarkson had dedicated his life to the Abolitionist cause and had undertaken considerable, detailed research talking to slavers and ex-slaves and writing extensively on the subject. He gave talks all over the country, including in places known to Jane Austen such as Bath, highlighting the issues and illustrating his talks with visual aids such as shackles and African goods showing that better trade opportunities existed.

One of Jane's favourite writers was the poet William Cowper, who wrote numerous poems such as *The Negro's Complaint* opposing slavery. Among his most well-known poems is *The Task*, which includes the words:

> We have no slaves at home – then why abroad?
> And they themselves, once ferried o'er the wave
> That parts us, are emancipate and loosed.
> Slaves cannot breathe in England; if their lungs
> Receive our air, the moment they are free,
> They touch our country and their shackles fall.

Another of her favourite writers, Samuel Johnson, had a Black manservant, Frances Barber. Barber had been enslaved in Jamaica, before being brought to England by his master Richard Bathurst, who later freed him. He then went to work for Johnson, before serving in the Royal Navy and ultimately returning to work with Samuel Johnson. Barber's son Samuel became a Methodist lay minister.

When visiting Bath, Jane would have been aware of the presence of people such as William Wilberforce and Josiah Wedgewood, who visited the city on several occasions. Josiah Wedgewood's iconic Society for the Abolition of Slavery emblem showing the image of a chained slave with the words 'am I not a man and a brother' could be purchased in Wedgwood's store in the centre of Bath.

Letters from Jane's brother Frank, a naval officer, would also have influenced Jane's personal views. In 1807, when Frank was serving in the Caribbean, one of his tasks was to enforce the 1808 Abolition Act – successfully capturing slave ships would result in prize money being granted to the officers and sailors. He commanded a ship that intercepted a Portuguese slaver, but as it was not an English ship, he was unable to stop it. Frank's letters to his family noted his disgust and revulsion for the slave trade, as well as the entire slave system.

Following a visit to St Helena in the Eastern Atlantic, Frank Austen wrote home comparing the different systems of slavery. He regarded slavery in St Helena as being relatively 'mild' compared to that of the 'harshness and despotism' common to the West Indies. In one such letter, Frank wrote 'the laws of the Colony not giving any other power to the master than a right to the labour of his slave. He must, to enforce that right, in case a slave prove refractory, apply to the civil power, he having no right to inflict chastisement at his own discretion.'

Despite this milder treatment, Austen is adamant that slavery was wrong. He went on to write, 'This is a wholesome regulation as far as it goes, but slavery however it may be modified is still slavery, and it is much to be regretted that any trace of it should be found to exist in countries dependent on England, or colonised by her subjects.'

As to Jane Austen's own views on the subject, there is no specific information available beyond general indications that she was sympathetic to the Abolitionists' cause and the brief references in *Mansfield Park*, *Emma* and *Sanditon*. One of Jane's letters to her sister Cassandra revealed her interest in Abolitionist literature as she refers to her love for the writings of Thomas Clarkson. It is quite possible that she encountered William Wilberforce in Bath, as he stayed in Great Poulteney Street in 1802, at the same time as Jane and her parents were seeking to rent property in the area. Wilberforce was regarded as a celebrity and would have visited places like the Pump Room on a regular basis.

Writing in *The Real Jane Austen*, Paula Byrne comments, 'It may not be coincidence that many of Austen's characters names – including Willoughby, Wickham, Lucas and Williams – are the same as those of West Indian plantation owners.'

Interest and sympathy towards the cause of the anti-slavery movement continued among members of the Austen family. In 1840, Jane Austen's older brother, Henry Thomas Austen, was named as one of two delegates from Colchester to the World Anti-Slavery convention. Attended by over 500 delegates, the convention was designed to work towards anti-slavery measures worldwide and to support former slaves who had been recently freed within the British colonies.

Chapter 14

A Propensity for Horror

Reading was a popular occupation in Jane Austen's time. Books were read individually or aloud as a social activity within a family or among a group of friends. In the 1790s, bookseller James Lackington noted in his records:

> The sale of books has increased prodigiously within the last twenty years. The poorer sort of farmers, and even the poor country people in general, who before that period spent their evenings in relating stories of witches, ghosts, hobgoblins, etc., now shorten the winter nights by hearing their sons and daughters read tales, romances etc., and on entering their houses you may see Tom Jones, Roderick Random, and other entertaining books stuck up on their bacon racks.

Books and newspapers were often shared between households. For many people the main problem was cost, as buying books could be expensive. The Reverend George Austen's personal collection of over 300 volumes was quite unusual given his financial circumstances.

As a result, libraries were well used. There were two types of library: a subscription library and a circulating library. Subscription libraries were not open to the public, and were mainly used by male subscribers who paid an annual fee which went towards purchasing more books. Each subscription library tended to focus on selected subjects such theology, travel, science and history.

Circulating libraries were more common. A typical advert for such a library was placed in the *Bath Chronicle* 1784. It stated that, for the cost of 10s 6d a year, or 4s a quarter, people could join the library in Cheap Street Bath as the owner had:

> opened a large Room up one Pair of Stairs (fronting the Church-yard) where they may amuse themselves with the NEWS-PAPERS and NEW PUBLICATIONS during the Intervals of drinking the Bath Waters, being very near the Pump Room ... He flatters himself it will be found a very comfortable Retreat, as it is covered with a Carpet, and a good Fire will be kept.
>
> Besides a select Collection of near SEVEN THOUSAND VOLUMES, including the most approved modern Publications, NEW BOOKS, Reviews, Votes of the House of Commons and ... NEWSPAPERS.

There were over 1,000 circulating libraries in existence by 1801. These libraries were basically business ventures that charged patrons a fee to borrow books for a specified period. They might be standalone businesses focusing solely on books, but many circulating libraries formed part of a wider business such as a haberdasher or tea and coffee merchant. Visiting a circulating library became a social activity, where ladies could exchange books, have a chat with friends, purchase ribbons and other sundries, thus making it an essential place to be seen during the social round in places such as Bath and London. In *Sanditon*, Austen refers to Charlotte buying 'new parasols, new gloves and new brooches for her sisters and herself at the library.'

The range of books on offer could be extensive in subject matter. Writing in 'Eighteenth-Century British Circulating Libraries and Cultural Book History', Edward Jacobs noted that in Darlington,

Co. Durham Mr Michael Heavisides operated a small circulating library containing just 466 books in 1,014 volumes of which:

> All types of fiction predominate, standard and cheapest contemporary types, many with the thinly veiled 'history' and 'memoir' titles ... Shakespeare's Poems (1 vol), Milton's Works, the Odyssey, Pilgrim's Progress and Holy Ward, translations of Lucan and Ovid, Knox's essays, Cook's Voyages, Spectator, Tatler, and Mirror, Smollett's History of England (10 vols.) Salmon's History of England (13 vols) Thompson's Poems, Rousseau's Emile, Berkeley's Minute Philosopher, Arabian Tales, and two apparently separate Persian Letters.

Publishers also operated circulating libraries, renting out their own books to the extent that, according to Lee Erickson writing in 'The Economy of Novel Reading: Jane Austen and the Circulating Library', the leading publisher of Gothic fiction became a 'wholesaler of complete, packaged circulating libraries to new entrepreneurs'. In addition, publishers began generating extra income by printing novels split into three volumes, renting each volume out separately. Henry Tilney in *Northanger Abbey* highlights this practice when he tells his sister Eleanor that 'Miss Morland has been talking of nothing more dreadful than a new publication which is shortly to come out, in three duodecimo volumes, two hundred and seventy-three pages in each, with a frontispiece to the first, of two tombstones and a lantern ...'

Jane certainly read novels. In 1807, she wrote in a letter to her sister Cassandra referring to Sarah Burney's *Clarentine*, revealing a change of heart about the story: 'I am surprised to find how foolish it is. I remember liking it much less on second reading than at the first and it does not bear a third at all. It is all unnatural conduct and forced difficulties, without striking merit of any kind.'

The growing popularity of novel reading was not always welcomed. James Fordyce's *Sermons to Young Women* noted 'What shall we say of certain books, which we are assured (for we have not read them) are in their nature so shameful, in their tendency so pestiferous, and contain such rank treason against the royalty of Virtue … that she who can bear to peruse them must in her soul be a prostitute.' While Samuel Johnson, writing in *Rambler No 4*, commented that 'these books are written chiefly to the young, the ignorant and the idle, to whom they serve as lectures of conduct, and introductions to life.' Thomas Gisborne argued that novels were addictive and 'secretly corrupted' women's minds, and that they should instead read improving books like those of William Cowper.

Jane Austen referenced such criticism in her novels. In *Pride and Prejudice*, Mr Collins was opposed to the idea of novel reading, while in *Sanditon*, Sir Edward Denham criticised both novel reading and the concept of circulation libraries, saying:

> The mere trash of the common circulating library I hold in the highest contempt. You will never hear me advocating those puerile emanations which detail nothing but discordant principles incapable of amalgamation, or those vapid tissues of ordinary occurrences, from which no useful deductions can be drawn. In vain may we put them into a literary alembic; we distill nothing which can add to science.

Austen also provided the reader with the opposite view, with Henry Tilney in *Northanger Abbey* saying, 'the person, be it gentleman or lady, who has not pleasure in a good novel, must be intolerably stupid.'

Foremost in the thoughts of critics who were opposed to novels, like Fordyce, were the proliferation of Gothic horror stories that were particularly popular with women. These were stories often regarded as indecent, promoting immoral behaviour and sinful thoughts. The Gothic novel style started in 1794, when *The Castle of Otranto* was published. It was ostensibly described as being a translation of a sixteenth-century document rediscovered in a house belonging to 'an ancient Catholic family in the north of England'. The real identity of the author soon surfaced; it was Horace Walpole, Earl of Orford, who was also an art historian and politician.

Gothic novels tended to be sentimental romances, sensational in style involving dramatic settings usually located overseas in Italy or Eastern Europe, or in the historical past, which created an immediate sense of strangeness. The books featured dark towers, castles and dungeons often located in wild, mountainous places, all shrouded in mystery. Heroines were young, beautiful and persecuted. Dangerous male characters abounded including tyrannical fathers, sinister monks, ghostly apparitions, and spectral voices. Hidden horrors were to be found round every corner. Ann Radcliffe, author of one of the most popular Gothic novels, *The Mysteries of Udolpho*, wrote that 'to the warm imagination the forms which float half-veiled in darkness afford a higher delight than the most distinct scenery the sun can show.'

It was a concept that reflected one of the popular art theories circulating at this time. Statesman and philosopher Edmund Burke postulated a theory of 'the Sublime and the Beautiful', advocating that there were two different art styles: the Beautiful, reflecting the pleasure of order, proportion, sunlight and calmness; and the Sublime, stressing 'delightful horror' involving darkness, terror, grandeur and savagery. This concept is best illustrated by the differences between the calm environments found in the work of artists Claude Lorrain, and the stormy, windswept, wild rocky landscapes of Salvator Rosa. There have been suggestions that the artworks of Salvator Rosa were a direct influence on Ann Radcliffe. Many of the scenic descriptions found in her novels appear to be based on Rosa's paintings.

Georgian families enjoyed visiting neglected ruins, seeking the picturesque and dramatic. A typical location was Netley Abbey, near Southampton, which was visited by Horace Walpole in 1755. He wrote:

> This little castle is buried from the Abbey in a wood, in the very centre, on the edge of the hill: on one side breaks in the view of the Southampton sea, deep blue, glistening with silver and vessels; on one side terminated by Southampton, on the other by Calshot castle; and the Isle of Wight rising above the opposite hills. In short, they are not the ruins of Netley but of paradise – Oh! The purple abbots, what a spot had they chosen to slumber in! The scene is so beautifully tranquil, yet so lively, that they seem only to have retired into the world.

It was a location that created the perfect atmosphere for lovers of the Gothic style: dramatic, surrounded by nature, mysterious and slightly spooky. There were hints of supernatural elements surrounding the abbey, with local people reluctant to visit at night even though there was talk of treasure hidden away. By 1775, Thomas Baker of Southampton included Netley in a guidebook with the words 'The beautiful effect of this ruin, and its surrounding scenery, is pleasantly developed in a poem of Mr Keate's entitled Netley Abbey, and a writer has chosen it as the theatre of a Gothic Story, in which the machinery of supernatural agency is agreeably managed, and the manners of the feudal ages well adhered to.'

Among the many appreciative visitors to Netley Abbey were members of the Austen family, including Jane herself.

The number of Gothic novels quickly proliferated, becoming easily accessible to a wide audience through the circulating libraries. Many of the authors of these Gothic novels were women. In 1798, a reviewer at the *Aberdeen Magazine* recommended that:

> Ye female scribes! Who write without a blot,
> 'Mysterious warnings' of – the Lord knows what;
> O quit this trade, exert your proper skill,
> Resume the needle, and lay down the quill.

This did not happen, however, as the theme has become an enduring one, albeit changing and transforming as the decades passed. During Jane Austen's lifetime, Gothic novels dominated reading habits, with readers exchanging books and recommendations among their contemporaries. Among those readers was Jane herself, who highlights the popularity of the genre among young girls in a conversation between Isabella and Catherine in *Northanger Abbey*, when Isabella declares:

> 'Dear creature! How much I am obliged to you; and when you have finished Udolpho, we will read the Italian together, and I have made out a list of ten or twelve more of the same kind for you.'
>
> [Catherine]: 'Have you, indeed! How glad I am! – What are they all?'
>
> 'I will read you their names directly; here they are in my pocket-book. Castle of Wolfenbach, Clermont, Mysterious Warnings, Necromancer of the Black Forest, Midnight Bell, Orphan of the Rhine and Horrid Mysteries. Those should last us some time.'
>
> 'Yes, pretty well; but are they all horrid? Are you sure they are all horrid?'
>
> 'Yes, quite sure; for a particular friend of mine, a Miss Andrews, a sweet girl, one of the sweetest girls in the world, has read every one of them.'

Looking at these titles, all of them feature the key elements of the genre: dramatic settings, unpleasant male characters, heroines forced to take action and solve mysteries in order to marry the man they love. In Eliza Parson's *The Castle of Wolfenbach*, the heroine Matilda Weimar runs away from her lecherous uncle and finds refuge at the Castle of Wolfenbach, then while exploring the building discovers the horrifying mystery of the missing Countess of Wolfenbach. To take another example, in Regina Maria Roche's *Clermont* the plot centres around the character of Madeleine. For many years she has lived a secluded life with her father Clermont, whose mysterious past has meant they have lived away from society. One stormy night, a mysterious countess arrives. She has links to his mysterious past and takes Madeleine away to live with her and be educated. Madeleine's life becomes a nightmare when she is attacked by thugs and assaulted in a gloomy crypt, then told she must marry a sinister stranger or have her father's past revealed. In order to marry the man she really loves, De Sevigne, Madeleine has to find ways of dealing with her unwanted suitor, save her father, and solve the mystery surrounding the countess.

Only two from Isabella's list are written by male writers: *The Necromancer; or, The Tale of the Black Forest* by Lawrence Flammenberg and Carl Grosse's *Horrid Mysteries*. Both focus on the activities of male characters within a Gothic setting. In *Horrid Mysteries*, Don Carlos and his friend, a marquis, become entangled in the activities of a secret society intent on achieving world domination. The heroes flee the society and death is constantly lapping at their heels throughout their subsequent adventures as they combat the society. *The Necromancer; or, The Tale of the Black Forest* contains echoes of a trend that develops into a wider horror sector. Centred around the activities of Volkert the Necromancer, it is a collection of linked stories involving murder, ghosts, horror and black magic.

Jane's familiarity with the concept and its style of writing can be seen in her novel *Northanger Abbey*. The book contains all the key characteristics of Gothic horror but are given a distinct Austen twist, thus becoming almost a parody of the style. Her heroine is an innocent girl in love with Gothic mystery stories who possesses a healthy imagination and is invited to stay in a spooky abbey. The location provides the perfect setting for Gothic horror, with hints of mysterious characters. Attempting to behave like a Gothic heroine, Catherine Morland is continually disappointed, such as when she anticipates finding hidden horrors within Mrs Tilney's room only to discover that it looks like any other bedroom. She unlocks a mysterious cabinet expecting it contain something horrible – only to find it is laundry bill. On another occasion, Catherine becomes convinced that the general has murdered his wife and tries to investigate, only to be caught by Henry Tilney and scolded.

Unlike typical Gothic heroines, Catherine Morland lacks experience, perception and understanding of other people. She does not know how to read people and identify reality from fiction and is forever bringing her love of the Gothic to everything she sees, hears and encounters, resulting in being constantly disappointed when reality does not match her dreams. She does not recognise Isabella's true nature until it is too late, nor does she appreciate and understand the relationship developing between James and Isabella. The key male character, Henry Tilney, continually teases Catherine about her love of Gothic and horror, such as when he creates a fictitious, humorous story based around Gothic links to Catherine's first night in Bath. As a result, the novel becomes a story showing Catherine learning to expand her horizons, becoming more aware and understanding about the reality of life.

Gothic novels continued to develop and grow in popularity in subsequent decades, with new ideas and writing styles such as that of the Brontë sisters and Bram Stoker transforming the original concept. In the late twentieth century, Jane Austen and her characters became themselves creatures of horror.

During the 1980s, 1990s and 2000s, vampires, zombies and other horror creatures proliferated in all forms of the media from books to TV, with series such as *Buffy the Vampire Slayer*, *Twilight* and *Vampire Tapestry*. Searching for ideas, writers turned to well-known classic stories and created new offshoots, new versions and generally transforming them. This practice ranged from fairy stories to classics such as *Pride and Prejudice*.

One of those writers was Regina Jeffers, author of *Vampire Darcy's Desire*, who claimed she had sought to maintain the main elements of the storyline in *Pride and Prejudice*, but turned Darcy in a Dhampire (a mythical creature resulting from the union of a vampire and a human) and Wickham into a vampire. In order to marry Elizabeth, Darcy has to break the 200-year-old curse upon his family rather than inflict the horrors of his undead life on her. As a result, they are 'forced to confront the seductive power of forbidden love, while dark forces are at work all around them. Most ominous is the threat from George Wickham, the purveyor of the curse, a demon who vows to destroy each generation of Darcys.'

By far the most well-known of this genre is Seth Grahame-Smith's *Pride and Prejudice and Zombies*. Written in 2009, the book came about as a result of a publisher making a suggestion about the possibility of combining *Pride and Prejudice* with zombie fiction. It was a concept that immediately appealed, with Grahame-Smith stating, 'You have this fiercely independent heroine, you have this dashing heroic gentleman, you have a Militia camped out for seemingly no reason whatsoever nearby, and people are always walking here and there and taking carriage rides here and there … It was just ripe for gore and senseless violence.'

Grahame-Smith's resultant novel combines the classic story, zombies and even ninja fighting! The plot starts with the outbreak of a zombie plague breaking out across the country. The Bennet girls attend a ball at Netherfield, but it does not turn out as planned after zombies attack the guests and the Bennet sisters use their martial arts skills to help keep people safe. Various other zombie attacks occur throughout the novel, with the girls and Mr Darcy thwarting each attack. The story eventually ends when Lady Catherine de Burgh challenges Elizabeth to a duel, which the latter wins. Even though the novel has a happy ending when Mr Darcy and Elizabeth get married, the risk of a zombie apocalypse still remains.

Pride and Prejudice and Zombies became a best-selling novel and was eventually adapted as a graphic novel by Del Ray, and later an interactive e-book. An app-based computer game was created, described as 'a rollicking action title with the perfect blend of zombie slaying and touching romance narrative.' The concept resulted in the publication of a prequel, *Pride and Prejudice and Zombies: Dawn of the Dreadfuls* and a sequel, *Zombies, Dreadfully Ever After*. The original was also made into a feature film in 2016 starring Lily James and Sam Riley.

The concept of mixing the conventional Jane Austen storyline with zombies and horror aroused considerable interest within the publishing sector leading to similar books appearing such as *Sense and Sensibility and Sea Monsters*.

Conclusion: Jane Austen's Legacy

Over 200 years since they were first published, Jane Austen's novels have remained enduringly popular, appealing to generations of readers. Outwardly, they are light-hearted stories about girls seeking husbands, but they also possess hints of something darker, something much deeper to be explored linking them to the wider society in which they lived.

These were girls who had little choice; if they did not find a husband, then the consequences could be dire. With no dowries and brought up as gentlewomen, they faced the risk of ultimately living in poverty, becoming a governess or companion or living on the charity of family members and having to accept being used as an unpaid governess or helper when required. Jane herself experienced this problem throughout her life; with no dowry, her marriage prospects were bleak. Although a close friend of Anne Lefoy, a marriage between Jane and Anne's relative, Thomas Langlois Lefoy, could not be encouraged because he had no money. Practicalities took precedence over love and affection.

It was not just young girls who faced such problems. Younger brothers who did not inherit land and title had to make their own way in life, usually via the Army, Navy, clergy or one of the professions – providing there was some money or connections to help them on their way. This is clearly seen in the careers of Jane's brothers, with only Edward being fortunate enough to be in a position where he inherited land and status. Jane's other brothers, Henry, Charles and Frank, all had to make careers of their own. Even then, poor decisions, partly due to the way in which people were dependent on social contacts, eventually led Henry into bankruptcy, a factor which had repercussions for the rest of his family.

In view of Jane's family connections and the work of her father, it would have been hard for Jane to be completely unaware of the issues within the wider world in which she lived. Her father, an educated clergyman, received newspapers at home and similar publications would have been readily available in the various circulating libraries used by Jane. Her cousin Eliza de Feuillide sought refuge at Steventon parsonage after her husband was sent to the guillotine during the French Revolution. Letters from Jane's brothers, especially Frank, reveal a steady flow of information about the conditions under which they lived, the difficulties experienced in developing their careers, as well as the places they visited such as the West Indies and its involvement in slavery. Jane knew all too well that as naval officers, their lives were constantly in danger whether from the conditions on board ship or during naval battles. Henry's Militia unit was involved in a mutiny, and as a serving officer, Henry was required to oversee the punishments. Some years earlier, Jane's cousin Eliza was caught up in a London riot during which her coach was attacked and her driver injured.

Disease was rife and death was never far away. At school in Southampton, Jane caught typhus and spent eighteen months convalescing. Meanwhile, her friends Mary and Martha Lloyd caught smallpox. Visits to Bath were often linked to attempts to find cures for illnesses like gout by taking the waters or by going sea-bathing, while common ailments were often assuaged with laudanum, which could easily become additive due to the presence of opium within the mixture. On top of this, many women did not survive childbirth.

There are hints too about issues of medicine, law, justice as well as wider concerns about ethical considerations surrounding slavery. Dark-skinned sailors were a frequent sight within naval towns like

Southampton, while numerous mixed-race children were sent back to England such as Nathaniel Wells and Dido Bell. Olaudiah Equiano travelled extensively around the country giving talks about the inequities of slavery, and Jane does make references to the abolition movement within her books. Regency society was undoubtedly more inclusive and ethnically varied than expected; these are not books that ignore the realities of society and life in the nineteenth century, but provide hints within the overall storyline.

One of the unusual elements within her books is the link to crime and the wider legal system. Jane's aunt, Mrs Leigh-Perrot, seems to have had a penchant for taking objects that did not belong to her and was accused of stealing lace, resulting in her being imprisoned and facing the threat of transportation. Such a threat to her future wellbeing was definitely possible, leading her husband to explore ways of dealing with his business so as to accompany her if necessary. It was even suggested that Jane and Cassandra should be present at the trial to support their aunt. Even a visit to London to stay with Henry Austen resulted in other encounters with serious crime.

There is one element of crime that can be found in all of Jane Austen's stories and has proved to be one of the key elements within her writing legacy. Indeed, modern crime writers have pointed out that the concept of a female detective can be traced back to Jane Austen, especially *Northanger Abbey* and the actions of Catherine Morland. Susan Zlotnick of Vassar College, USA is a specialist in nineteenth-century writers and believes that Catherine Morland was:

> one of the earliest girl detectives in the literary canon, an eighteenth-century Nancy Drew snooping into drawers and ferreting out criminal behaviour … As foolish as Catherine's searching for a hidden manuscript may be, it challenges the domestic status quo and calls upon the heroine to act heroically: to demonstrate strength, bravery and self-determination.

Elizabeth Veisz, Associate Professor of English at Bridgewater State University, Massachusetts agrees. Writing in '*Northanger Abbey*, Gothic Parody and the History of the Fictional Female Detective' for the Jane Austen Society of North America, she points out that the novel is very much a 'precursor to female-detective and girl-sleuth literature' and that such 'Quixotic gothic parodies lay the foundation for later female-centric mystery literature'. According to Professor Veisz, it shows the heroines searching out material evidence conflicts between how they approach their conclusions as opposed to what others want them to see. Most importantly, she believes that 'these narratives establish a character type explicitly counter to the traditional gothic heroine, paving the way for indefatigable lady detectives and adventurous girl sleuths in the later nineteenth and twentieth centuries.'

Mystery writer Stephanie Barron, who has written several stories set in Georgian times featuring Jane as a sleuth, puts the case for a slightly different view of the detective element within *Northanger Abbey*, linking it into the perennial issue of the role of women in society. She writes: 'At the heart of *Northanger Abbey* is the chief mystery, central to all of Austen's work: a young woman's effort to penetrate the veil between herself and – rather than Laurentina's skeleton as Catherine imagines – the male half of her world.' Barron believes that Catherine does not take on the role of chief detective within the story, instead she 'plays Watson to Henry Tilney's Holmes. It is Henry who uses his intelligence and expertise to finally confront the novel's chief "suspect" (his father, General Tilney) and figure out the motive for the General's "crime" (ejecting Catherine from Northanger Abbey with such malicious haste).'

Barron told the Jane Austen blog that she believes one of the reasons leading to Jane's enduring popularity is her observational skills:

> I believe that one reason we return again and again to Austen's novels is due to her profound understanding of the human

> heart – or in criminal terms, human motivation. She shows us constantly how people manipulate others to get what they want; how they assume masks and deceive; how the women in her stories must in fact be detectives solving the riddle of the men before them – about whom they know very little, and must penetrate the truth of their characters because those man and their motives may determine happiness or misery for the rest of the heroine's lives. Jane was a natural detective, and she lived in an era when there was no formal police force. Everyone was an amateur in her world.

The intricate relationships and complex storytelling found within Jane Austen's novels have even led to suggestions that Jane Austen herself possessed all the skills necessary to become a successful crime writer. The crime novelist P.D. James wrote that '*Emma* is a wonderful detective story and the clues to the real relationships are most cleverly planted. I think that if Jane Austen were writing today, she might very well be our greatest mystery novelist.'

Once you start looking, it becomes very clear that Jane was extremely intelligent and observant. As the anonymous reviewer in *The British Critic*, a literary journal published in 1818 pointed out:

> Her characters, her incidents, her sentiments, are obviously drawn exclusively from experience … she seems to have no other object in view; than simply to paint some of those scenes which she herself has seen, and which everyone, indeed, may witness daily.

> Her heroes and heroines make love and are married, just as her readers make love, and were or will, be married … She seems to be describing such people as meet together every night, in every respectable house … And to relate such incidents as have

> probably happened, one time or another to half the families in the United Kingdom.

The reviewer concludes by saying:

> She makes her dramatis personae talk; and the sentiments which she makes them use, strike so familiarly upon our memory as soon as we hear them repeated, that we instantly recognise some of our acquaintance, the sort of persons who she intends to signify, as accurately as if we heard their voices … Her merit consists altogether in her remarkable talent for observation; no ridiculous phrase, no affected sentiment, no foolish pretension seems to escape her notice.

The reasons why Jane Austen and the Regency period attract such enduring interest are not hard to find. Jane dealt with themes that possess perennial interest: romance, marriage, money, power, and status and wrote stories that are engaging, lively and reflect human character. Her powers of observation were acute, noting human foibles and highlighting them within her stories. Jane's work reflects society, both now and then, in all its frailties, faults and values, whether good or bad. It is perhaps one of her greatest strengths because there is always something familiar to be identified. Recognising her skill, many modern authors have picked up on that aspect of her work, using the well-loved characters to further stress the resulting problems in a way that even young children can appreciate. One portrayal aimed at youngsters even shows Mr Darcy as a proud duck who comes to tea with a group of female ducks – the Bennet sisters. Pride leads Mr Darcy to fall into an enormous puddle full of thick squelchy mud and has to be rescued by Lizzie.

Jane's books feature themes and storylines that echo across the years simply because they are of universal concern. Her ability to observe, note and to analyse meant that she was able to use her storylines to reflect the darker elements of life which are forever present, particularly women's rights and how issues of health, education and finances impact on family members. Life in Georgian England was not easy, no matter what your status in society; the risk of death, illness, and poverty was always present.

This was a period of change and transformation in the role of women, as well as industry, society, transport and the wider world. Even in Jane's lifetime women had begun to gain greater freedom; she is later able to travel on her own to London by stagecoach – something that would have been unthinkable for a single woman even ten to fifteen years earlier. Alongside these changes are the constantly present darker elements of the Georgian lifestyle. No matter what your status in society might be, making a mistake could be fatal, whether it related to marriage prospects, a place in society, or a career. Sheer desperation forced many young women such as Jane's aunt Philadelphia to risk their lives and travel thousands of miles in the hope of finding a husband and place in society among total strangers.

Jane's novels do not ignore the realities of society and life of the period, but put them into context of the life of a family without detracting from the storyline. This is a world that still speaks to us across the centuries, featuring issues that continue to influence and dominate our lives.

Her novels, combined with the extensive knowledge of her background and lifestyle revealed through her letters and the accounts of other members of her family, as well as the objects in her possession, shine a light into the deeper, wider society that existed during the late eighteenth and early nineteenth centuries. The result is a legacy that is constantly influencing and encouraging readers to explore her world, both that of the light-hearted social round and the darker elements that are constantly in attendance.

Resources

The Jane Austen Centre www.janeausten.co.uk
Jane Austen's World www.janeaustensworld.com
Jane Austen Society of North America www.jasna.org

Almeroth-Williams, Tom, *Syphilitic City*, University of Cambridge, 2020

Bennett, Michael, 'Jenner's Ladies: Women and Vaccination against Smallpox in Early Nineteenth-century Britain' *Journal of the Historical Association*, Vol 93, No. 4 (312) October 2008

Borer, Mary Cathcart, *Willingly to School: A History of Women's Education*, Lutterworth Press, 1976

Breihan, John, 'Jane Austen and the Militia', Jane Austen Society of North America, Persuasions #14, 1992

Byrne, Paula, *The Real Jane Austen: A Life in Small Things*, Harper Press, 2013

Bruyn Andrews, C. (ed), *The Torrington Diaries containing the Tours through England and Wales of the Hon. John Byng (later Fifth Viscount Torrington) between the Years 1781 and 1794*, Barnes and Noble, 1970

Caplan, Clive, 'Jane Austen's Soldier Brother: the Military Career of Captain Henry Thomas Austen of the Oxfordshire Regiment of Militia 1793-1801', Jane Austen Society of North America, *Persuasions* #18, 1996

Day, Malcolm, *Voices from the World of Jane Austen*, David & Charles, 2006

De Courcy, Anne, *The Fishing Fleet: Husband Hunting in the Raj*, Weidenfeld & Nicholson, 2012

Fullerton, Susannah, *Happily Ever After: Celebrating Jane Austen's Pride and Prejudice*, Frances Lincoln, 2013

Fullerton, Susannah, *Jane Austen and Crime*, Jane Austen Society of Australia, 2005

George, M. Dorothy, *London Life in the Eighteenth Century*, Penguin Books, 1925

Gerzina, Professor Gretchin, *Britain's Black Past*, BBC Sounds, 2016

Hall, Edward, *Miss Weeton: Journal of a Governess*, Oxford, 1939

Hickman, Katie, *She-Merchants, Buccaneers and Gentlewomen: British Women in India,* Virago, 2019

Kedzie, Dr Robert C., *Shadows from the Walls of Death*, 1874

Le Fay, Deirdre (ed), *Jane Austen's Letters*, Oxford University Press (fourth edition), 2011

Martin, Joanna (ed), *A Governess in the Age of Jane Austen: The Journals and Letters of Agnes Porter*, Hambledon Continuum, 1988

Milligan, Barry, 'Morphine-Addicted Doctors, the English Opium-Eater, and Embattled Medical Authority', *Victorian Literature and Culture*, Vol 33 No. 2 (2005)

Purdie, D.W., 'The Maladies of James Boswell, Advocate', *Journal of the Royal College of Physicians of Edinburgh*, Issue 32, 2002

Richardson, Kirsten, *The Season: A Social History of the Debutante*, W.W. Norton & Co., 2020

Scott, Arthur Finley, *The Georgian Age (Everyone a Witness series)*, Martins, 1970

Tomalin, Claire, *Jane Austen: A Life*, Penguin Books, 1997

Wilson, Bee, *Swindled: From Poison Sweets to Counterfeit Coffee*, John Murray, 2009

Worsley, Lucy, *Jane Austen at Home,* Hodder & Stoughton, 2017

Index